What does God like better than a Golden Temple?

Why were the People mean to Jeremiah?

How can God use Me?

_____

From

_____

Date

_____

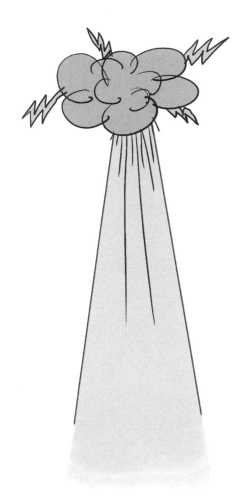

DAVID

Drops a Giant Problem

And Other Fearless Heroes

DAVID

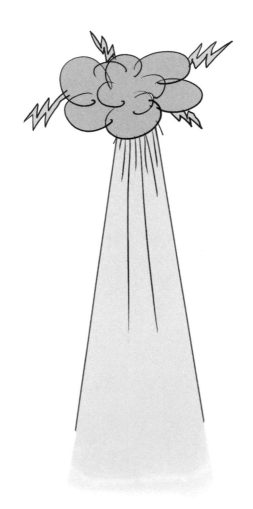

Drops a Giant Problem

And Other Fearless Heroes

JILL & STUART BRISCOE
pictures and cartoons by **RUSS FLINT**
music by **LARRY MOORE**

Baker Books
A Division of Baker Book House Co
Grand Rapids, Michigan 49516

Text copyright 1997 by Jill and Stuart Briscoe
Music copyright 1997 by Larry Moore
Art copyright 1997 by Russ Flint

Published by Baker Books
a division of Baker Book House Company
P.O. Box 6287, Grand Rapids, MI 49516-6287

Printed in the United States of America

Library of Congress Cataloging-in-Publication Data

Briscoe, Jill.
    David drops a giant problem : and other fearless heroes / Jill and Stuart Briscoe : Russ Flint, illustrator.
      p. cm.
    Summary: Retellings of stories from the Old Testament about Samuel, David, Solomon, Jeremiah, Daniel, and Jonah are accompanied by "Let's Pretend" stories, "Neat Facts," plays, and songs.
    ISBN 0-8010-4216-X
    1. Bible stories, English—O.T. Historical Books.
2. Bible stories, English—O.T. Hagiographa. 3. Drama in Christian education. 4. Bible plays. [1. Bible stories—O.T.] I. Briscoe, D. Stuart. II. Flint, Russ. III. Title.
BS551.2.B746 1997
221.9'505—dc20   96-38564

An accompanying tape (ISBN 0-8010-3017-X) is available from the publisher. It features a children's group singing all the songs in the four books and the Briscoes reading selections from the "Let's Pretend" and "Let's Make a Video" sections.

This book is produced in cooperation with Alive Communications, Inc., 1465 Kelly Johnson Blvd., Suite 320, Colorado Springs, CO 80920.

CONTENTS

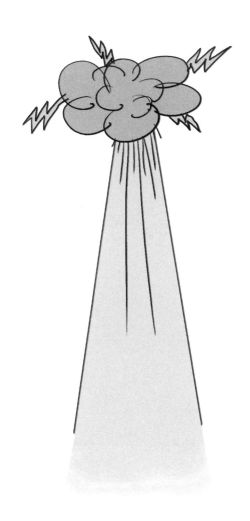

We gratefully appreciate the following people who made this project a delight.

Betty De Vries, a wise and skillful editor, whose vision for a children's book coincided with ours and whose skill far exceeded our abilities.

Kappie Griesell, who so diligently dug out the Neat Facts.

Larry Moore, who took our words and added his delightful music that sets our feet tapping and our hearts singing.

Russ Flint, whose art is so entrancing and interesting that we wonder if anyone will read our text.

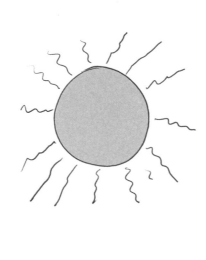

To
our grandchildren,
whom we love so dearly

May this book
bring delight to your hearts
and more love
and appreciation
for the God whom we serve.

There's something special about this book

 To

catch by surprise
and to surprise with joy
freshen
and excite new attention
in the old, old story

 To

peek around the corner of a verse
and delight to see
who is coming

 To

smell the smells
admire the rich clothes
and glimpse the colors
of worlds different from ours

 To

break the bread of life
into small enough pieces
for young minds
to thoroughly digest

 To

tell of Jesus—
from Genesis to Revelation

 To

discover truths old and new
young and old
child and adult
together

To

experience
with laughter and tears
simple retelling of old
stories allowing
imagination to refresh
favoriteevents using songs
and simple dramas to promote
understanding

 To

know God better
love God more

 To

share these discoveries
with a lost, hurting world
of children
and adults

To

this end
authors
artist
composer
publisher

invite you to enjoy
Book 2, *David Drops
a Giant Problem:
And Other Fearless
Heroes*!

Letter to Parents

Now that our three children are in their "thirty somethings," we realize we have been parents an aggregate of over a hundred years.

There's more!

As our children have produced nine grandchildren, at last count, we have accumulated almost forty years of grandparenting.

So you could say we have a vested interest in children.

We enjoy telling stories to youngsters, answering their questions, hearing them laugh, and watching their eyes light up with understanding. There's nothing quite like a fire, a cozy chair, a child, an adult, and a good children's book.

"Read us a story, Papa Stu," elicits a special response, especially when you have a good story available.

"Tell us about Daniel and the lions, Grandma," will energize even a fatigued senior citizen.

With these things in mind, we started to work on this project. We wanted to produce something that would convey the old, old story in a new and fresh way. Our intention was that children, long familiar with Bible stories, would be drawn to them once again because they were presented differently. How differently? Well, we are firm believers in children having their own imaginative capabilities and their special brand of humor. So "straight stories" are immediately followed by imaginative, humorous "Let's Pretend" tales.

Parents may be surprised to learn that Jonah's whale was called Wally and that the seagulls observing his watery excursion were called Bea Gull and Dee Gull, and that mountains talk to giraffes, but children will take it in their stride. And they'll love Russ Flint's pictures and cartoons and funny little sketches. They'll laugh and so will you.

Our primary aim is to lead young children and adults alike to a wider knowledge of the Book of Books. May you find these books interesting, endearing, entertaining, educational, and inspiring.

Happy reading,

Jill and Stuart

The twelve historical books follow the Pentateuch, the first five books of the Old Testament. These twelve books tell the story of the Israelites and how God dealt with them as they lived in the land of Canaan. The Book of Joshua tells about the struggles the Israelites had entering the land. The Canaanites who lived there were very wicked people. God said they had to be removed, but that was not easy to do. When the Israelites did not do what God commanded, there were all kinds of problems.

When God's people began to do what the wicked people were doing, God was very unhappy. So he provided leaders called judges to teach the people God's ways, to lead them in battles against their enemies, and to be judges so that the people could live safely and wisely. The Book of Judges tells about these things.

The most famous judge was Samuel. Two books of the Bible have his name. Samuel was a good man, but his sons, who were supposed to be judges like their father, were wicked. So the people asked Samuel to give them a king like the other nations had. Samuel said this was not a good idea because God was their king. But the people insisted, so God said Samuel should go ahead and anoint Saul as Israel's first king. Saul started out as a good king but soon began to do wrong things. God chose David to be king in Saul's place.

David wanted to build a temple for the Lord to replace the old tabernacle (tent church). But God had a different plan. God wanted David's

THE BOOKS OF HISTO

son Solomon to build the temple in Jerusalem. When David and Solomon were Israel's kings, the nation became rich and strong.

When Solomon died, the people rebelled against his successor, and the kingdom was divided. The northern part, called Israel, was ruled by Jeroboam, and the southern part, called Judah, had King Rehoboam.

As the years went by, Israel and Judah had many kings. Some were good, but many were bad. God sent prophets to warn the kings and the people that they were displeasing him, but the people would not listen. Later both Israel and Judah were defeated by their enemies, and the people were taken from their homes into captivity in other lands. All these stories and many more are told in the Books of Kings and Chronicles.

When people are forced to live away from their homes, we say that they have been exiled. So this time in the Bible is called the exile. God did not leave his people. He sent prophets to speak to them. After about fifty years, the captives were told that they could return to Jerusalem if they wanted to. Many of them did. They set about the difficult task of rebuilding their destroyed cities and particularly the ruined temple. Two of their leaders were called Ezra and Nehemiah. We read the exciting story of their struggles and eventual success in their books.

Next are the two small but important books of Ruth and Esther. They tell the stories of two outstanding women who loved God and served him.

SAMUEL

A nice woman named Hannah lived in Israel. She lived with her husband, Elkanah, and his other wife, Peninnah, who had a lot of children. (Men had more than one wife in those days.) But Peninnah was jealous of Hannah because Elkanah favored her. Peninnah knew Hannah wanted a baby very much and would make fun of Hannah because she had no children. This hurt Hannah deeply.

Every year the whole family went to Shiloh to worship God at the tabernacle. Once when they were there, Hannah prayed really hard to God to give her a baby. She told God that if he answered her prayer and her baby was a boy, she would give him to Eli, the high priest. Then her son could grow up and learn how to serve the Lord in the tabernacle at Shiloh. Hannah's prayer was answered, and she named her son Samuel, which means "asked of God."

The little boy grew up and Hannah loved him very much indeed. It was hard to keep her promise to God and take her little boy to Shiloh where he would live. But Hannah knew that there Samuel would learn how to serve the Lord, and that was the most important thing to learn in the whole wide world.

When Samuel was still quite small, Hannah and her husband went to Eli at the tabernacle and left Samuel in the old priest's care. Eli was very kind to him, and Samuel learned all sorts of things as he grew up. He helped Eli and listened to him teach the people about God. Samuel slept in a special room near the holy place where the ark of the covenant was kept. The ark was the gold-covered chest where Moses had put the two blocks of stone on which God had written the Ten Commandments.

Samuel got to see his mother only once a year. Every time Hannah would come, she would bring a beautiful coat. She had spent months making it just right. Samuel wore a tunic, a very plain white garment—something like a long V-neck tee shirt. All the priests wore a tunic. When Samuel wore the beautiful embroidered coat over his tunic, he felt very, very special.

One night, when Samuel was twelve years old, he was in bed asleep when a voice awakened him: "Samuel, Samuel." Samuel thought it was Eli's voice, so he got up quickly and ran to him. But Eli was fast asleep. Samuel woke him up gently and said, "Here I am."

"I didn't call you," said Eli. "Go back to bed." So Samuel went back to bed.

After this had happened three times, the old priest sat up and suddenly had an idea. Maybe God was calling Samuel because he wanted to give him a message. "Samuel," he said to the young boy who was standing there looking quite worried, "maybe God is calling you. Go and lie down, and if you hear the voice again, say, 'Speak, Lord, for your servant is listening.'"

So Samuel ran to his bed and lay down. He knew God had talked directly to Eli, because the old man had told him about it, but Samuel also knew it had not happened for a long time. When he heard the voice again, "Samuel, Samuel," he replied, "Speak, Lord, for your servant is listening."

God told Samuel that Eli would soon stop being the head priest and

Eli and his two sons would die because the sons did wicked things and would not pay attention to their father. Samuel was frightened. God was telling him something serious indeed. The voice came straight from heaven and now Samuel knew what was going to happen to Eli and his two sons. Samuel was frightened because he didn't want to lose Eli, but he was also frightened for another reason—he didn't want to tell Eli what God had said to him.

In the morning Samuel got up quickly and began to do all his duties. He kept out of Eli's way and hoped Eli would not ask him about the message from God. But the old man looked for him and asked Samuel to tell him. At first Samuel didn't answer Eli's questions, but the old priest told Samuel he had to, and Eli wanted to know everything God had told Samuel. So Samuel bravely told Eli everything God had said. When Samuel had finished, the old man sighed a deep sigh and said, "God must do whatever he wants to. He knows what is right."

From that time on, Samuel began to hear God's voice clearly. God would give Samuel a message, and Samuel would tell the people what God had said. Eli and his two sons died just as God had told Samuel they would. But God's people knew that, even though they had lost their priest and leader, God had chosen Samuel to be their new leader.

All his life Samuel loved and served God. The Lord did many wonderful things through Samuel.

Let's **Pretend**

THIS IS A STORY TOLD AS FANTASY MARRIED TO FACT TO BE MIXED WITH FAITH AND LAUGHTER, LOVE AND JOY.

I CAAAAN'T HEEEEEEAR YOOOOOU!

THE SOLDIERS AND THE SPIRIT

Samuel had anointed David secretly. Only David's family knew about it and that was just as well. Samuel had made Saul king years before God told Samuel to go and anoint David. So it was all very awkward.

Saul thought he was still king even though he knew something dreadful had happened inside his heart. Saul had not been an obedient king. He had done things that God had told him he was not to do. So God took away his Spirit from Saul's heart and gave the power to be king to David.

Saul knew God's Spirit had left him and was sorry about it. But God did not change his mind. God told Samuel he had chosen David to be king instead of Saul.

You know how icky you feel when you've had a place on a sports team and then someone comes along and is given your place? Then you just have to sit and watch instead of playing? That's how Saul felt. When he saw how brave David was, killing giants and many enemy soldiers, Saul became jealous. After God's Spirit left Saul, he found out he was afraid of giants. Saul decided he would try to kill David.

"Commander of my army!" he shouted.

"Yes, your majesty," the commander answered, coming quickly into the king's presence.

"I have heard that David is hiding in Samuel's town. In fact, I believe David is actually with Samuel and Samuel is protecting him. That makes me angry indeed. Take your soldiers and go and get David and bring him to me."

"Yes, Sir!" answered the commander.

1 Samuel 3:9

Speak, LORD, for your servant is listening.

So off he went with his men.

When they got to the place where Samuel was, they saw that Samuel and his followers were having a prayer meeting. David was nowhere to be seen. The soldiers were getting ready to search for David when suddenly they all began to join the prayer meeting. They couldn't help themselves. Even the commander found himself praying. They prayed instead of searching for David.

When Saul heard about this, he called for another leader in his army.

"Go and capture David," he said. "David is in Samuel's town hiding out."

The second group of soldiers set off. When they got to Ramah they saw all their buddies praying and praying and suddenly God's Spirit came on them too and they all joined in!

Saul heard about that too. He was very angry. After all, he had sent his men to capture David, not to pray. So he sent a third group. And would you believe it, they couldn't stop themselves from joining the prayer group either.

"I've never seen anything like this in my life," said David, watching from his hiding place.

Samuel said to David, "Come on, let's

escape and go to Naioth (a place nearby). Maybe Saul will give up and stop chasing you." So they left all the praying soldiers and made their escape.

"There's only one thing left to do," Saul raged when a messenger came and told him what had happened. "I'll go myself and get him."

So Saul set off. He asked people along the way, "Have you seen David and Samuel?"

"They are at Naioth," the people told him.

As Saul walked toward the place where David and Samuel were, he suddenly found himself on the ground praying. He tried to stop, but he couldn't! People heard him praying because he was praying loudly. They said, "Maybe Saul is going to ask Samuel if he can be a prophet instead of a king!"

Suddenly Saul saw Samuel standing right in front of him. Saul knew David must be very near by. Saul tried to stand up but he couldn't because God wouldn't let him. So Saul lay on the hard ground all day while David escaped from the town and ran away to hide in the hills.

This was the way God protected David.

When Samuel lived, the ark of the covenant was about four hundred years old and was in the tabernacle at Shiloh where Joshua had placed it. That was where it belonged. Once it was taken out of the tabernacle when it should not have been and lots of trouble happened. Many people suffered or died because the ark was in the wrong place.

When the Israelites were losing a battle against the Philistines, some Israelite soldiers thought if they took the ark of the covenant (a symbol of God's presence) into the battle, the Philistines could be easily defeated. God was angry with the Israelites and allowed the Philistines to capture the ark. Many Israelites were killed in the battle.

The Philistines moved the ark three times: to Ashdod, to Gath, and to Ekron. In Ashdod they placed the ark in the temple of their god, Dagon. What a mistake that was! The next morning, Dagon had lost his head and his arms. God was

telling the Philistines something. What do you think it was?

Next the Philistines moved the ark to the city of Gath. God sent those people, young and old alike, a plague of tumors.

The people of Gath quickly sent the ark to the city of Ekron, but the Ekronites didn't want trouble. They were afraid they would be killed. So the ark was sent back to Beth Shemesh in Israel. The Philistines sent five gold rats and five gold tumors along with the ark as a guilt offering to God.

Seventy men who lived in Beth Shemesh looked inside the ark (the ark was a holy thing and was not to be touched by the people), and God became so angry with them that they died.

So the people of Beth Shemesh didn't want the ark in their city either. They sent it on to Kiriath Jearim where it remained in Abinadab's house for about twenty years.

Samuel & Me

Sometimes the things God asks us to do are very hard. It was hard for Samuel to tell Eli what God had told him. Samuel didn't want to hurt Eli. Samuel didn't want someone he loved to be upset with him. But Samuel told Eli everything because that was the right thing to do.

It is a good thing to tell the truth. It's *always* the wisest thing to do, even if sometimes it upsets people you love.

Sometimes we can go to church a lot—just like Samuel did. He was in church "all" the time. Even though we go to church a lot, that doesn't mean we know God personally. The Bible says, "Now Samuel did not yet know the Lord" (1 Samuel 3:7). There came a time when he heard God speaking to him and he came to know God for himself. Do you know God personally? Ask your mom or dad to help you—or if they don't know how to help—ask your pastor or Sunday school teacher.

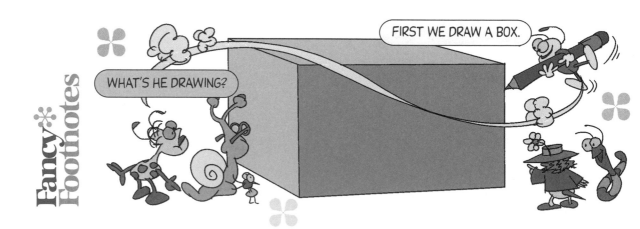

Let's Make a Video about

I CAAAAN'T HEEEEEEAR YOOOOOU!

OOOH WAA WAA DOO WAPP SHA-NA-NA.

Your Family Video Theater

God Looks at the Heart

Cast: voice of God, Samuel, Jesse and wife, eight sons, one or two servants

Scene: Samuel sitting on his bed, holding his head.

Voice of God	Samuel, Samuel—
Samuel	Speak, Lord, your servant is listening.
Voice of God	What's the matter with you?
Samuel	I have such a headache—
Voice of God	The trouble is in your heart, not your head. How long are you going to go about with such a long face? King Saul has disobeyed me, and I have rejected him as king.
Samuel	But I had such high hopes for him, Lord God. He is like my own son.
Voice of God	There is a man whom I have chosen to be king instead of Saul, and I want you to go and anoint him.
Samuel	But . . . but Saul would be angry with me if I did that. He . . . he might even kill me.
Voice of God	Yes, he will be very angry with you. So you'll need to go about it very carefully. The feast days are fast approaching.

WOOOOOOSH

THEN WE MAKE A LID AND WE DRAW GOLD RINGS ON THE SIDE.

ABOUT 3 MINUTES.

YOUR SON IS GOOD. HOW LONG HAS HE BEEN DRAWING?

27

Go to Bethlehem, and if people ask you why you have come, say you have come to lead their festival. Then go to Jesse's house and take your horn filled with oil to pour over the head of the new king. That is to show I have chosen him to be king. So, go, Samuel, and anoint this person.

Samuel   Who is this king you have chosen? Jesse has eight sons.

Voice of God   I will tell you who it is when you get there.

Samuel   I will do as you say. I will go, Lord.

It is mealtime at Jesse's house for Jesse, his sons, his wife, and his servants. Samuel stands front stage, with meal being prepared behind him. Servants set the table.

Samuel   I'm confused, Lord. Jesse's sons are all able, intelligent, brave young men. It's going to be very hard to choose the right one.

Jesse   *(greeting Samuel, bows)* We are honored to have you lead our feast, Samuel. Sit here, if you will, in the place of honor. *(Samuel sits at head of table. Sons line up to meet him.)* This is my firstborn, Eliab. *(Samuel gets horn and oil ready.)*

Voice of God   Don't look at his height, Samuel. Look at his heart! This is not my king. *(Samuel and Eliab disappointed. Eliab sits down at end of table with back to Samuel. Next son, Abinadab, bows to Samuel.)*

Abinadab   I am Abinadab.

Two other boys pushing and shoving in line.

Voice of God   Not this one, Samuel. He looks in the mirror at his own face instead of looking into mine.

Samuel   *(Third son, Shammah, comes to Samuel.)* Then what about this one, Lord?

Shammah   My name is Shammah. I am a brave warrior.

WE DRAW POLES THAT SLIDE THROUGH THE GOLD RINGS TO CARRY THE ARK.

ZIIIP

WHAT'S INSIDE THE ARK?

Voice of God	And a proud one! He thinks his own strength is all he needs to fight his battles. He doesn't bother to depend on me.
Samuel	*(as next son, with scroll in hand, bows)* See, Lord, this one carries the Scriptures.
Voice of God	Yet, he never reads them. What good does it do to carry my Word around if it is never read? He is trying to impress you, Samuel.

Three more sons come in a group to the prophet. Samuel talks to them for a few minutes.

Samuel	Lord, this one tells me he gives large amounts of money to the poor. Surely he would make a good king.
Voice of God	Man sees only what he gives; I see only what he has left. *(Boy jingles large money bags hanging on his belt, and boys move to side to watch last boy, the seventh, approach Samuel.)*
Jesse	*(to Samuel)* This boy is a good boy. He always does as I tell him. He says, "Yes, Father," when I ask him to do his Friday duties.
Voice of God	Yet, as soon as his father's back is turned, he grumbles and complains. He doesn't like being a servant. He could never be a king.
Jesse's wife	*(pleading)* My Lord, this one is my favorite. He's popular with everyone.
Voice of God	That is true. He is a people pleaser, not a God pleaser. He wants everyone to like him so much he will do anything they want him to, even if it is wrong.

Samuel	(turning his back on last son) Lord, is this the king then? There are no more—

Last son behind Samuel's back makes faces, some of his brothers laugh. Jesse's wife cuffs him on ear. Samuel turns and sees what is happening.

Samuel	(to Jesse) This . . . cannot be the one. Why, he mocks me! Do you have any more sons?
Jesse	Only the youngest, who keeps my sheep in the fields.
Samuel	Send for him. We will not sit down to eat until he comes. (All groan.)

Enter David. Brothers look in amazement and anger at him.

Voice of God	This is the one I have chosen. Man looks on the outside, but God looks on the heart. Anoint him, Samuel. While others see a shepherd boy, I see a king.

David kneels and is anointed by Samuel.

Speak, Lord

Words and Music by
JILL BRISCOE and LARRY MOORE

Not too fast

1. 2. Speak, Lord, Your servant is listening. Speak, Lord, so
3. Speak, Lord, Your servant is listening. Speak in my

I hear Your word._____ Speak to my heart and soul,
joy and my pain._____ Speak in my darkest hour,

3rd time to Coda

touch me and make me whole,
give comfort, peace and pow'r.

Speak, Lord, Your

There are five books of poetry, sometimes called the "Wisdom" books in the Old Testament. These books tell us what God's people were thinking and feeling as they lived through the experiences we read about in the earlier books of the Old Testament.

The Book of Job tells the story of a rich and noble man who had many terrible things happen to him. Job had some friends who were not helpful because they did not understand why God was allowing these things to happen to Job. Later, Job understands that God is still in charge and loves him even though life has been very difficult. Job thanks God for being so good.

The word *psalms* means "songs." It is helpful to think of the Book of Psalms as a collection of 150 different songs that God's people sang when they felt like singing or that they used in their worship services. David wrote many psalms but other people wrote psalms too. Some of the psalms were written when the writers were going through difficult times and others were written to show how happy the people were. So we have happy psalms and sad psalms. When the people of God walked long distances to the temple together, they liked to sing to help them on their way. A lot of the psalms were written for this purpose. Many psalms tell stories about what God did in the old days. Some of the psalms talk about what God will do in the future. So there are psalms for all kinds of different situ-

THE BOOKS OF POET

ations. Even today many people sing the psalms in church or at other times. That helps them tell God what they think about him and how they are feeling about life.

Proverbs are very short sentences that are easy to remember. There are many things God does not want us to forget because they are so important. So we have a book called Proverbs that is full of easy-to-learn and hard-to-forget important things. All of us need to know how to behave: what to do and what not to do. The proverbs are helpful because they quickly tell us what to do. Many people do not like to listen to long talks. They like to get their information quickly. The Book of Proverbs is a good place for them to begin learning what God wants them to know and what they need to do about it.

The Book of Ecclesiastes was written by someone who knew that people want to be happy, but many of them aren't. The writer told about many of the things that people do to be happy. He also wrote about the reasons for their unhappiness. He reminded people that they will be happy only if they live the way God says they should.

The Song of Songs is the story of a simple country girl. When the king saw her, he sent for her because he wanted to marry her. But she had a boyfriend whom she loved. So she did not want to marry the king. She went back to her boyfriend. This is a story about love and faithfulness that reminds us of God's love for us and our love for him.

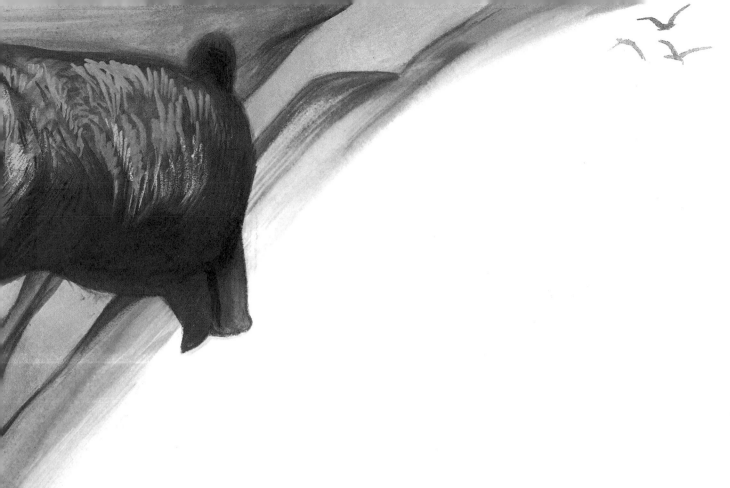

DAVID

When David was a young boy, his father gave him the job of looking after the sheep. This meant that David helped the sheep to find fresh water and grass. Because the land was hot and dry, this was not easy work. When David had found the right place for the sheep to graze, he would give them time to eat and drink their fill and then quietly lie down and digest their food. As he kept his eyes open for animals that might harm his flock, David enjoyed the wonders of God's creation and worshiped the Lord in his heart.

Most shepherd boys learned to play a musical instrument—a pipe or a flute, or a harp. David was a very good harpist and he could sing. As he thought about God and his creation, David wanted to offer thanks to God, so he made up little poems and sang them to tunes he made up on his harp.

After he had defeated the Philistine giant, Goliath, David became a close friend of King Saul's son, Jonathan. David was often a guest of the royal family and sang some of his songs for them. Sometimes King Saul got depressed, and at times it seemed that only David's music helped him. But that didn't always work either. Once King Saul threw his spear at David while David was singing. Fortunately, David saw it coming and ducked. He got out of there in a hurry.

David became popular in Israel not only because of his songs but also because he was a successful soldier. The people began to like him more than they liked the king, and this made Saul unhappy. He did many bad things to David and Jonathan, and there were many days when David was in great danger

and had to run away and live in caves in the wilderness. But even then he wrote songs and poems about his experiences. They were, of course, quite sad.

When David became king, he did many good things, but he was not perfect. He also did some bad things, but he admitted them to God and was sorry. He even wrote songs about the experience of doing things that were wrong, being sorry, and being forgiven by God.

More than anything else, David wanted to build a temple for the Lord in Jerusalem. It was called the city of David because he built it up as the new capital of the nation of Israel. The ark of the covenant needed a better home than the old tabernacle. But David had been a soldier and God did not want him to build the temple. David's son Solomon, who would someday be a king of peace, would be allowed to do it. David was disappointed about this, but he began collecting things that would be used when the temple was built.

The most important room in the temple would be the Holy of Holies, the place for the ark of the covenant. Since the ark had been captured by Israel's enemies and then returned many years before, the Israelites had not been too interested in it because they weren't interested in God. David found out where it was stored and arranged for it to be brought to Jerusalem in a great procession. He wrote some special music for the event. Then he had the choirs and the trumpeters and harpists and all the other musi-

cians learn the music, which they sang and played as loudly as they could. David was so excited that he led the procession. He threw off his royal robes and danced with joy. The crowds thought this was great, but his wife didn't think it was proper behavior for a king. So he got into a lot of trouble when he got home.

David wrote all kinds of songs: worship songs, happy songs, sad songs, songs for special events, songs for processions, songs to be sung by individuals, songs to be sung by choirs, and songs for all the worshipers. We still sing them today because like David we are sometimes happy, sometimes sad, sometimes thankful, sometimes sorry, sometimes worshiping alone, and sometimes worshiping in church with other people. Wherever there are people who want to sing to the Lord, they will always find songs in David's psalms.

The LORD is my shepherd. Psalm 23:1

Let's Pretend

DON'T YA EVER **TAKE A BREAK?**

SALLY THE SHEEP

It was a cool, starlit night on the hills outside the town of Bethlehem. A young shepherd boy sat on a rock where he could see the sheep lying contentedly around him. He was playing softly on a simple harp. The music he made filled the air. The sheep liked to hear him play. His pleasant sounds and soothing words calmed them after a hard day of clambering over the rocky hills in search of nourishing, fresh grass. Sally the Sheep was especially glad to hear the music. She baa-ed in response. "I hear you, Sally," said the shepherd boy, interrupting his song. He knew Sally's special baa. In fact, he knew every sheep so well that he could recognize them even in the dark by their voices. They knew his voice too.

Sally licked her legs, which showed signs of wounds. Her head had been torn too. The wounds were healing slowly. The shepherd boy had poured oil into them after he had bravely rescued her from a mountain lion. She had wandered just a little too far away from the rest of the flock while the shepherd boy climbed down a craggy cliff to rescue another sheep that had fallen. The lion waited patiently while the shepherd reached and hooked the sheep with his long, crooked staff. Then the lion pounced on Sally, tearing at her wool, and dragged her toward his lair. Sally had baa-ed out in fright. The shepherd boy came running and wrestled the lion to the ground, giving Sally the

chance to run away. Sally had heard an older sheep tell how the shepherd boy had done the same thing for her when a bear had attacked. With a stout wooden club studded with sharp bits of metal—also called a rod—he had fought off the bear. Sally took great comfort in knowing the shepherd boy's rod and staff were always there to protect her from harm.

After the attack, Sally had not been able to walk far, but the shepherd boy had taken her and the other sheep to a quiet brook where, under the shade of the trees, she had been able to lie down and gain back her strength. Sally had been afraid to wander more than a few feet away from the shepherd boy for a long time. But his quiet confidence had begun to restore her soul, and as the days went by, she began to be less fearful. Somehow the shepherd boy's music was bringing all these thoughts back to Sally's mind. She loved the shepherd boy deeply. Chewing contentedly on a fresh piece of grass, she rose quietly and walked over to the rock where the shepherd boy was sitting. She listened to the sweet music of his harp and began to hum-baa to herself while she thought these thoughts:

This boy is my shepherd,
I shall not lack,
He makes me lie down in green fields
And leads in the proper path.

David, the shepherd boy, smiled gently at Sally the Sheep and then began to sing with a clear, strong voice. It was as if he had heard what she was thinking. He sang:

The Lord is my shepherd, I shall not be
    in want.
  He makes me lie down in green
    pastures,
he leads me beside quiet waters.

STUFF NEAT STUFF NEAT

David killed
Goliath. Did you know
Goliath had four brothers
who were also giants? In his
lifetime David and his men
fought and killed the other four
giants too.

41

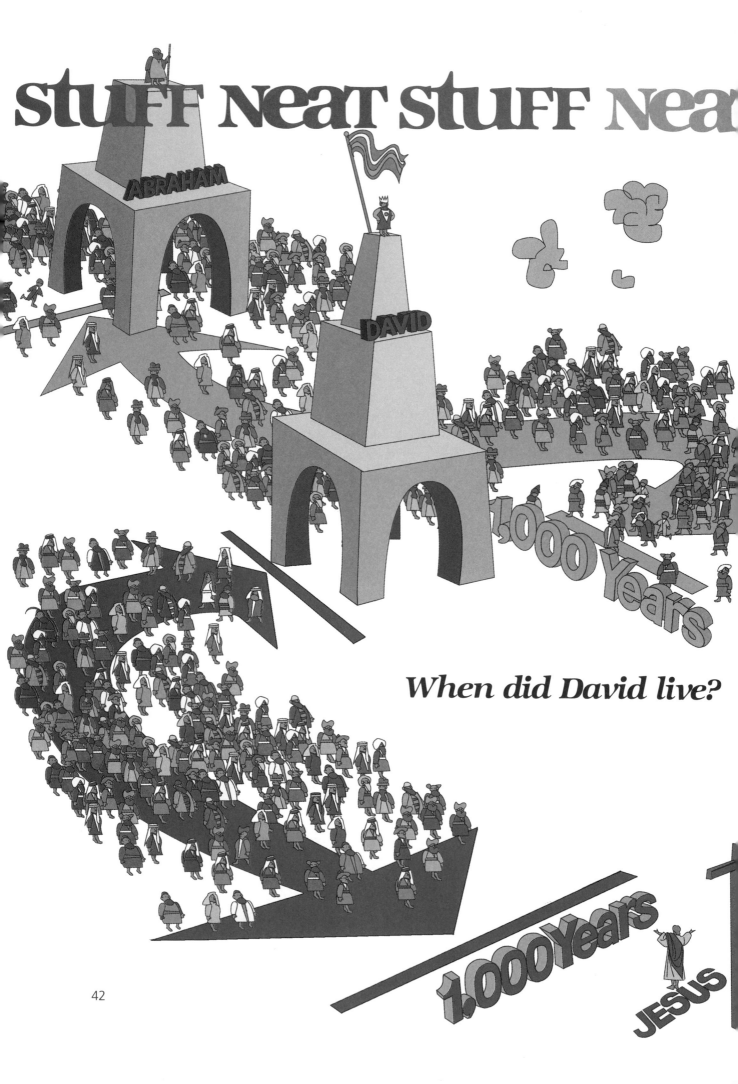

When did David live?

42

What jobs did David have during his lifetime?

shepherd   poet   city planner
musician   soldier   businessman
songwriter   general   king

What words describe the kind of person David was?

After you learn more about David maybe you can add other words to the list to describe him.

courageous

clever

awesome

handsome

Fair

friendly

humble

prayerful

faithful to God

sensitive

strong

loyal

43

David & Me

Where do you come in your family? Are you the oldest, middle, or youngest child? Sometimes when you are the youngest child, like David, your brothers and sisters may tease you, leave you out of their games, or think you are not as important as they are. God thinks you are in just the right place in your family and in his family. He has some special things that only you can do.

SHEPHERDS PROTECT THE FLOCK AND KEEP THEM TOGETHER.

DAVID FOUGHT THE PHILISTINES, TOO.

WHO WERE THE PHILISTINES?

THEY WERE MEAN, WAR-LIKE PEOPLE WITH FEATHERS IN THEIR HELMETS.

THE PHILISTINES USED A LOT OF IRON IN THEIR SPEARS AND CHARIOTS MANY YEARS BEFORE THE ISRAELITES DID.

Fancy Footnotes

COME ON. WE'RE GOIN' FOR A WALK.

Let's Make a Video about

Your Family Video Theater

Nadir, the Shield Bearer

David

Cast: Goliath, Nadir, and David

Scene: Outdoor area with brook running through center. Nadir and Goliath on left; David on right.

Goliath	Are you ready, Nadir? It's time to go.
Nadir	Just finishing polishing your shield, Sir.
Goliath	Polish it brightly, my boy, so it will dazzle my enemies.
Nadir	I will hold it before you, Sir, to protect you from the fiery darts of the champion of Israel.
Goliath	*(laughing)* Champion of Israel? They don't have a champion. They're all afraid of me.
Nadir	I'd be afraid too, Sir. You are so big and strong. I'm glad I'm on your side. I'm glad I have to carry your shield before you.
Goliath	Come with me, boy. We'll stand on the hilltop and challenge them to come and fight.
Nadir	I think it's a great idea that you and their champion should fight instead of both armies fighting. It will save a lot of people from getting hurt.
Goliath	It's also a great idea because it means we'll always win. No one beats Goliath.
Nadir	I wonder if anyone will come to fight today.
Goliath	We'll soon see. *(lifting up his voice)* Come on, you wimpy Israelites. Send out your man and let us fight.
David	Just a minute, Goliath. I'm not quite finished picking stones from the brook. I'll be with you in a minute.

Nadir	Who said that? I can't see anyone. Oh, yes. Look, Sir, in the brook at the bottom of the hill. It's a young boy. What is he doing?
Goliath	He's coming this way. It must be some kind of joke.
Nadir	Anyone joking with you, Sir, must have a strange sense of humor.
David	I'm not joking, Nadir. You'd better keep out of the way if you don't want to get hurt.
Goliath	What is the meaning of this, boy? Go back to your mother before something nasty happens to you.
Nadir	Yes, go home, my friend. My master is a strong man with a long spear and a nasty temper.
David	I've warned you, Nadir. You go back to your mother, because Goliath will fall today.
Goliath	Enough of this talking. Why are you here, boy?
David	I'm here to get you, Sir. You have become a nuisance to the people of God, and I have volunteered to get you out of the way.
Goliath	If I get my hands on you, boy, I'll tear you apart and send you home in little pieces to your mother.
David	No, Sir, I plan to go home in one piece. I have come here because God has sent me, and he will look after me. You are very big, Goliath, but your arms are too short to fight with God.
Nadir	I don't like the way he's talking, Sir. He has a strange look in his eye. Maybe he knows something we don't know. Perhaps he is keeping you talking while his brothers steal up on you from behind. I can't protect you from the front and the rear, Sir.
David	This is your last warning, Nadir. I'm telling you to get out of the way.
Nadir	It's my job to protect my master. I cannot move out of the way. Anyway, what weapons do you carry that could possibly do my master harm?
David	I have one sling and five stones.
Goliath	Five stones? Boy, we're talking war here. We're not playing games.
David	I have five stones, Sir. One for you and one for each of your four brothers, should they be foolish enough to show up.

Nadir	He's swinging his sling around his head, Sir.
Goliath	He'll need more than a sling and a stone, boy. Keep up the shield. I don't want my armor getting scratched with one of his little stones.
Nadir	I've never seen anyone swing his sling so fast, Sir. Look out, Sir, the stone's coming!
Goliath	A stone you say? What can a stone do to me?
Nadir	Sir! It flies so high into the sun, I can't see it to protect you from it.
Goliath	No fear, boy. Ahhhhhh!
David	Good shot, eh, Nadir? Your master lies dead at your feet. Now go home.
Nadir	I think I will, unless you need a shield carrier. I'm out of work now, you see. Or on second thought, could you teach me how to swing a slingshot?

SOLOMON

Imagine being the wisest person in the world. What would that feel like? What kinds of responsibilities would such a person have?

Who was the wisest person who lived during all the time of the Old Testament? Solomon. One can't be as clever as he was unless God makes a person like that. One night Solomon, who had just become king of Israel, had a dream. It was no ordinary dream, for while Solomon slept, God came to him. God said, "Ask me for anything you want and I will give it to you."

How exciting that must have been!

One of Solomon's big jobs would be to decide who was right when two people who each wanted their own way asked him to settle their arguments. Solomon asked God to give him understanding of the people and their problems so he could make wise and fair (what the Bible calls "just") decisions. God liked his prayer and made Solomon the wisest king who ever lived. God also promised Solomon riches and honor, two selfish things he could have asked for but didn't.

For a long time Solomon did what was right and used the wisdom God had given him to help others. He wrote three thousand songs and made up over one thousand clever sayings called proverbs. Solomon also taught about mammals, reptiles, fish, birds, and plants. To him the natural world was God's world, which he loved, so another part of his wisdom was that he knew much about God and his world. He was like a walking encyclopedia.

Solomon was not perfect and made many mistakes. He had too

Would you like wisdom or lots of money?

many servants, had turned some of the people into slaves, had taxed the people too heavily, and had too many wives—about one thousand. He had too many horses and chariots in his army, which God had said Solomon would trust more than he trusted God.

Solomon had started out doing everything very well. He began by loving and serving God as his father, David, had done before him. But Solomon didn't keep it up. Again God visited him in a dream. It was kind of God to warn him to stop doing things he had been told not to do, mainly not to worship any other god but the Lord. Many of Solomon's wives had come from

other lands and worshiped different gods. Solomon wanted to please them, so he worshiped their gods too. In his old age Solomon loved and listened to his wives more than he loved and listened to the Lord. God rejected Solomon for this reason and said that in his son's lifetime God would take the kingdom away from Solomon's family and give it to someone else.

King Solomon did many wonderful things while he loved and obeyed God, and he was wise and successful. But when he stopped being wise and obedient and began to do many unwise things, his life was ruined and he became very unhappy.

Let's Pretend

THE GREATEST KING OF ALL

THIS IS A STORY TOLD AS FANTASY MARRIED TO FACT TO BE MIXED WITH FAITH AND LAUGHTER, LOVE AND JOY.

THERE NOW, LIE DOWN AND **RELAX.**

The queen of Sheba heard about Solomon. She heard how clever he was, how rich he was, and how beautiful were the buildings he had built. She couldn't believe all she had heard. "I don't believe anyone can be as clever as all that," she said to her prime minister.

"People say it is all true, your majesty," the prime minister replied.

"Well, I don't believe it," the queen said. "And unless I see it for myself, I won't believe."

"Why don't you go to Jerusalem, your majesty? You could take some rich treasures along with you so Solomon can see how rich you are. While you are there you can ask him some really difficult things to see if he can answer you. If he can't, you'll know all you've heard isn't true, and you can show him you are more clever than he is!"

The queen of Sheba liked the idea. She didn't like people always telling her about how wonderful King Solomon was. She really thought she was the greatest person in the world. So the servants began to pack up all the things they would need to travel from the queen's kingdom to Solomon's.

The queen had to go a long, long way to see Solomon, but she was determined to impress the king, so she ordered her servants to load the camels up high. "I want dozens and dozens of camels in a very, very long procession," she told

them. When it was time for all of them to set off, the people ran out of their houses to watch. They couldn't believe their eyes. "Look at all the jars of spices on the camels," a boy cried.

"Never mind the spices; look at all the boxes of gold and jewels," cried another.

After a long time, this queen from the south arrived at Solomon's palace, called the Palace of the Forest of Lebanon. She took one look at it and nearly fainted. It was far, far bigger than hers! It had taken Solomon thirteen years to build, so you can imagine how large and beautiful it was. Once the queen of Sheba got inside the palace, she couldn't believe how huge the rooms were. One room was called the Hall of the Forest of Lebanon. It was 150 feet long, 75 feet wide, and 45 feet high. That's nearly four times as high as our ceilings. Four rows of cedar pillars held up the roof in the great room. The queen of Sheba began to count the windows. "There are forty-five of them!" she gasped. It was the biggest room in the whole country, and the queen felt small when she stood in the center of it. "I've never seen such a wonderful palace," she said to her chief servant. He nodded in agreement.

When the queen saw King Solomon sitting on his magnificent gold throne in his royal throne room, she didn't know what to say. She gave him her wonderful presents, and King Solomon said thank you. Then he told his servants to pack up the empty camels with presents he wanted to give her. King Solomon's presents were even more rare and precious than the queen's, and there were so many of them the camels' knees began to give way under the weight.

"Everything I have heard about you is true," the queen told Solomon. "But I have some problems I want you to solve."

"Tell me what they are," said Solomon, "and I'll try to give you some answers."

We don't know what problems the queen of Sheba asked the king about, but she may have asked him about things like why God lets people we love get sick and die, or why there are so many poor people in the world who don't have enough food to eat. Or maybe she wanted to know why some people are smarter and can do their homework more quickly than others. Perhaps she wanted him to explain why some people are extra beautiful or extra mean. Whatever they were, the Bible says she asked Solomon a lot of hard questions, questions no wise man had even been able to answer in her country. Solomon was so wise he answered every single one of them and got all the answers right the first time.

After the queen had all her questions answered, had eaten all the foods she was served at the huge banquets Solomon put on for her, had seen all the splendid uniforms that Solomon's officers wore, and had counted up all his hundreds of servants, she felt faint all over again.

"How great is your God who has given you all of this!" she exclaimed. "He has made you the wisest, richest, most wonderful king in all the earth. You are even greater than the greatest queen. It must be wonderful to live here in Jerusalem, to be one of your wives or servants who continually hear your wisdom! I must go back to my people and my country. I will tell everyone in my part of the world that your God is the greatest God of all. And because he loves Israel he made you a king who makes good laws and fair decisions that are helpful to all your people."

So the queen of Sheba returned to her own land, believing that Solomon's God was the only God in the whole wide world who should be worshiped and that he is the greatest ruler of all, even greater than Solomon.

Remember the tabernacle Moses and the people of Israel carried with them in the desert? After King David built himself a beautiful palace, he wanted to build God a beautiful temple to take the place of the tabernacle. When he talked to God about his idea, God said that David could collect the stone, cedar wood, bronze, and gold. But David could not build the temple. That was a job God wanted Solomon, King David's son, to do.

Thousands of men, both Israelites and people who lived in other countries, worked for seven years building the temple. They cut and smoothed the heavy stones and shaped the cedar logs before the pieces were hauled to the building spot. No sound of hammering or sawing was heard as the temple was being built.

The inside of Solomon's stone temple looked almost like the inside of the tabernacle. It had the same rooms and the same pieces of furniture. But the walls and ceilings were carved with cherubim (angels), palm trees, fruit, and open flowers. All the walls were carefully overlaid with gold.

Do you know anyone with a horse? Even one horse takes a lot of looking after and needs feeding and exercising regularly. Solomon had 40,000 stalls for chariot horses and 12,000 horsemen to drive those chariots.

Have you ever written a song? If you have, you know how hard it is. Solomon wrote 1,005 songs.

Do you have a job? Perhaps you have a paper route or get money for babysitting. Imagine doing those things and getting paid not with dollars but with food! The men who worked for King Solomon got paid for the work they did with sacks of cracked wheat and barley, barrels of wine and olive oil, and fresh fruit.

Some of us are interested in cats. Some of us know a lot about football. Others like to read about people who did brave things. Solomon was interested in *everything*.

Solomon & Me

God doesn't want us to do the right thing only once or twice or even a dozen times. Solomon started his life serving God, but Solomon ended his life serving himself. That's not good! God wants us to go on doing what he says all of our lives. Do you find it hard to finish what you start? Can you think of one thing you started but haven't finished? What was it?

Solomon asked God to help him with his work and God did. God will help you with yours too.

When you pray, try to ask for the most important things and not just the things you would like to buy or play with. What would be one of the most important things you would like to ask God for?

Ask him to make you kind to your sisters and brothers, for example. Ask him to help you to be polite and caring about others, or to help you tell other kids at school about Jesus and how they can know him too. God always likes to hear you pray prayers like that and will be sure to answer them.

It is always easier to listen to people we can see rather than listen to God, who we can't see. Practice listening to God by reading a little bit of his Word every day of your life. Never stop. Let's not disappoint God the way Solomon disappointed him.

Let's Make a Video about

PARTICIPANTS ARE ENCOURAGED TO EXPAND AND IMPROVISE, USING THIS MATERIAL AS A GUIDE. ALLOW YOUR IMAGINATION TO "PEEK AROUND THE CORNER OF THE VERSE" AND SEE WHO IS COMING.

YA SOUND MUCH BETTER. THAT REST HELPED.

Your Family Video Theater

Two Mothers, One Baby

Cast: Solomon's servants Asa and Aram, Leah and Tamar, Solomon

Scene: Room in Solomon's palace.

Asa	How clever do you think King Solomon is?
Aram	Well, he's *so* young, but we'll soon see how clever he is today. He has a really sticky problem.
Asa	What's that?
Aram	Well, there's a court case he's to judge. There are two women coming to see him. They are arguing about a little baby.
Asa	Oh, I heard about that. Each says the baby belongs to her. The women want Solomon to decide whose baby it really is!

Enter Solomon, two women, and baby.

Leah	Your majesty, we live together and both of us had babies born the same day. During the night this woman's baby died, and the next morning she took my baby away from me while I was asleep. So I want you to tell her to give me back my baby.
Tamar	*(clutching baby)* I didn't take her baby. It was her baby that died, and now she wants mine, and I'm not going to give him to her.
Asa to Aram	How can Solomon tell who's telling the truth? There was no one else there, so either of them could be lying.
Solomon	Silence in court! Each of you women tell me this baby belongs to you. One of you is obviously not telling the truth.

	So I'm going to find out which one of you is lying. Bring me a sword.
Aram	Yes, your majesty. Take mine. *(gives his sword to Solomon)*
Solomon	Both of you want the baby. So now I will divide the baby in two with this sword and give you each half a baby!
Leah	*(crying)* No, no, dear sir, give her the baby. Don't harm him—
Tamar	Go ahead and cut the baby in two. That way neither of us will have it.
Aram	How clever the king is! The one who is the real mother loves her baby so much she would do anything to save him, even give the child to the other woman. The threat to kill the child has shown us who is the real mother.
Solomon	Silence in court! Give the baby to the woman who has spoken up for him. She has shown us she is the real mother by her loving concern for the child's life.

The baby is given to his mother; exit mothers, baby, and Solomon.

Asa	Let's go and tell everyone in Israel what a clever young man the king is. God has given him a wise and discerning heart.

1 Kings 3:9

TLB

Prophets were very special people. God explained things to prophets so they could then tell the people what God wanted them to know. Prophets had to be very careful to hear what God said to them. Sometimes God told them things in dreams. He did this often for Ezekiel. Other times the prophets heard God's voice. This happened to Samuel. But we are not told how God let some of the others know what to say. The prophets were a great help to God's people. Prophets not only told the people what God wanted them to know but also gave the people hope and God's promises of being saved from their problems. The best promise, of course, was the promise of the Messiah.

Prophets like Isaiah were very close to the rulers of the land, so it was easy for them to give God's message to the leaders of the people. Other prophets, like Elijah, were hated by the leaders, and their lives were often in great danger.

Many of the things that the prophets did and said were written down either by the prophets themselves or by their followers. The last seventeen books of the Old Testament, called the prophetic books, contain these writings. The first five prophetic books were written by Isaiah, Jeremiah (who also wrote the Book of Lamentations), Ezekiel, and Daniel, who together are called the major prophets. The final twelve books are the books of the minor prophets. This does not mean that the books are not as important as the other five but only that they are shorter than the others. Their titles are Hosea, Joel, Amos, Obadiah, Jonah, Micah, Nahum, Habakkuk, Zephaniah, Haggai, Zechariah, and Malachi.

After Solomon died, the nation of Israel was divided into two parts, each with its own king. The northern kingdom was called Israel.

THE BOOKS OF PROP

The southern kingdom was Judah, and its capital was Jerusalem. For many years the kings quarreled and the people suffered. A few of the kings, especially of Judah, were good, but most did very wicked things and soon most of the people were also doing wicked things. This went on for over three hundred years. Finally God allowed Israel's enemies to overtake the kingdom of Israel, and the people were either killed or taken captive, never to return. The kingdom of Judah continued to exist, but often the people were very wicked.

Three times the Babylonians, who were the most powerful people in that part of the world, attacked the city of Jerusalem and finally destroyed it. Even Solomon's temple was ruined. All the temple gold and furnishings were carried off to Babylon. In 586 B.C. the rest of the country was captured. Almost all the people of Judah were taken from their homes and made to live in faraway lands. We call this part of their story the captivity or the exile. When the people were taken into captivity, God sent prophets with them. Ezekiel and Daniel were with the people to remind them about the reasons for their situation and what God had in store for them. The prophets were a great help to the unhappy people.

After seventy years, many of the people were allowed to return home to rebuild Jerusalem. This was very difficult work, but God sent his prophets to the people even there. The prophets kept reminding the people to finish the work God had given them to do. So God continued to speak to his people, but the people did not always listen.

God was interested not only in the people of Israel and Judah, but often gave the prophets messages for people of other lands. Once God sent his prophet Jonah to Nineveh to speak to the people there.

JEREMIAH

Jeremiah was very frightened. The Lord wanted him to be a prophet. Being a prophet was often dangerous. Prophets sometimes had to say things that people did not like to hear. God often told prophets to tell people they were doing bad things and should stop doing them. Sometimes the people got so angry with the prophets they threw stones at them. Some prophets were killed by angry people. Jeremiah knew this so he did not really want to be a prophet. He did not like the idea of having a job where people might hate him and throw stones at him.

God told Jeremiah that he had always wanted Jeremiah to be a prophet. Before Jeremiah was born, God knew what he wanted Jeremiah to be.

When Jeremiah grew up, he was very shy. He didn't like people looking at him and he didn't know what to say to them. Imagine his surprise, therefore, when one day the Lord told him, "I want you to be a prophet, Jeremiah!"

"Oh, not me, Lord," Jeremiah replied. "I'm no good at talking in front of people. I'm very young and nobody would listen to me, and I'm scared."

"I know all about that, Jeremiah," the Lord replied. "But my plans are the very best that anyone can possibly have. It won't be easy, but it will be the right thing for you to do. I will tell you what to say, and I will show you how to say it."

"But I will still be very frightened," Jeremiah said.

"Of course you will," said the Lord, "but I will be with you and will always look after you." So Jeremiah agreed to be a prophet and he was a very good one for forty-one years.

65

Jeremiah prophesied during the reigns of the last five kings of Judah. Most of his messages from God were to the foolish and bad leaders and priests in Jerusalem.

Jeremiah loved his country of Judah and wanted the best for the people. But his advice and warnings were not liked by the authorities, and they often treated him badly.

Once Jeremiah was speaking in the temple, and a mob of bad priests and false prophets wanted to kill him. Some of the elders spoke up for Jeremiah and convinced the people he should not die.

The first time the Babylonians besieged the city, they heard that the Egyptians were coming, so the Babylonians left to go fight them. Jeremiah started out for his home in the village of Anathoth a few miles from Jerusalem. The authorities arrested him because they said he was deserting to go over to the Babylonians. He was in a dungeon a long time before the king heard about it and released him.

Later a group of princes who really hated Jeremiah seized him and threw him in a cistern, a hole in the ground for holding rain water, that was full of mud. A friend told the king and got permission to rescue Jeremiah, and he was kept in the courtyard of the guards' barracks.

When Jeremiah predicted that the Babylonians would come back and win, he was accused of discouraging the defenders of Jerusalem. He was really warning the people that they could not hold out against the Babylonians and should not try to fight them if they wanted to live.

Just as Jeremiah had said, Jerusalem was at last completely destroyed. The king and his wicked advisors tried to flee, but they were caught and killed. The rest of the people, including Jeremiah, were made to march as captives to Babylon. But the Babylonian army commander found him and had him released from his chains. He said Jeremiah could go to Babylon as a free man or stay in Judah. The commander knew Jeremiah had prophesied honestly about God's plans.

Jeremiah chose to stay in his homeland. But some time later a group of country people decided to go to Egypt and they forced Jeremiah to go along. No more is known of his life.

Jeremiah had a helper who wrote down on a scroll all the prophecies Jeremiah had made in his many years as a prophet. That helper was called a scribe. When the king read that scroll, he became very angry and burned it. Jeremiah and the scribe made a new scroll and added more prophecies and that became a large part of the Book of Jeremiah—the book that has more words in it than any other book of the Bible.

Let's Pretend

ICKY, STICKY MUD

THIS IS A STORY TOLD AS FANTASY MARRIED TO FACT TO BE MIXED WITH FAITH AND LAUGHTER, LOVE AND JOY.

HEY, YOUR VOICE IS WEAK. YOU MUST BE HUNGRY.

When Jeremiah was a small boy, he liked to play in the mud. All small boys like to play in mud. One day he came home covered with mud, and his mother was very unhappy. She told him to take off his muddy clothes and stay in the house while she went outside and washed them. Jeremiah wanted to go out to play with his friends, but his mother said he must stay at home until his clothes were dry. He knew it would be a long time before that happened because the winter winds were blowing in the rain clouds, and the air was wet and cold.

When his mother had washed his clothes, she called him. "Come here, Jeremiah. You and I need to talk." Jeremiah did not want to talk because he knew that his mother was unhappy with him, but he was an obedient child so he went to her. His mother said, "Now, Jeremiah, I am very unhappy with you because you have been playing in the mud again."

Jeremiah replied, "All the boys play in the mud, Mother. Why can't I? Is it because it causes you more work? I'm sorry if that is the problem. I'll wash my own clothes if you'll just let me play with the other boys."

Jeremiah was surprised by her answer. "Jeremiah, it's not the extra work that I mind so much. The problem is you don't

seem to realize that the mud holes you play in are very dangerous." Jeremiah's mother had told him this before, but he didn't listen. So she asked his father to talk to him about the mud holes. Jeremiah listened then!

His father said, "Jeremiah, you know that in the summer we have very hot weather and no rain. But in the winter the rains come, and we need to collect the water so that we will have some in the summer months. We dig holes in the rock or in the ground and line them with stone. They are called cisterns. They fill up with water, which we drink until it is all gone and we look forward to the winter rains. Sometimes we dig new cisterns, and the old ones aren't used any more. When that happens, the holes fill up with icky, sticky mud. Now, if you fall in there, you might not be able to get out. That's why we don't want you playing in the mud holes, especially the cisterns."

Many years after this, when Jeremiah was a famous prophet, some of the men in Jerusalem were very angry with him. He had been saying things the wicked men did not want to hear. They decided on a plan to stop Jeremiah from talking. They really wanted to kill him but were afraid to do this. So they captured Jeremiah one day and took him into the courtyard of the barracks where the soldiers lived. In the center of the courtyard was a mud hole—an old cistern. It was very deep and smelly and full of icky, sticky mud. They grabbed hold of Jeremiah and put ropes under his arms. Then they began to lower him into the mud hole. The ropes hurt him as they slid

under his arms, but the men did not care. Down, down into the smelly darkness they lowered him until his feet touched the mud. Then lower and lower they dropped him. The mud came up to his knees, then his waist. "That's enough," said the men who were looking down at him from the edge of the mud hole. "Pull out the ropes and leave him there. That will teach him not to tell the people things we don't want them to hear."

With that they pulled the ropes out from under his arms. This hurt him even more than when they had lowered him down. But the men didn't care. Once the ropes had been pulled out from under his arms, Jeremiah began to sink even lower into the mud. Up to his chest he sank. Then he remembered the words of his parents. He realized that he was in a very dangerous position. He struggled to get out, but the more he struggled, the deeper he sank in the icky, sticky mud. "Help!" he cried at the top of his voice. His voice rang loudly in his ears as it echoed around the stone walls of the cistern. "Help me! I'm sinking in the mud," he shouted. The walls of the cistern echoed "mud, mud, mud."

The men who had put him in the mud hole went on their way laughing about what they had done. But a good man called Ebed-Melech overheard them. He ran to the king and told him what had happened to Jeremiah and asked the king for permission to get Jeremiah out of the mud hole. "Certainly," said the king. "Take thirty men with you. You'll need them to pull Jeremiah out of that awful, icky, sticky mud."

The thirty good men ran as quickly as they could to the cistern. "Jeremiah, are you there?" they called as they peered down into the dark hole.

"Yes, I'm here," he replied faintly, "but I'm sinking very quickly. Please hurry."

"We'll throw a rope down to you. Put it under your arms and all thirty of us will pull you out of that icky, sticky mud," the men said.

Jeremiah shouted, "My arms are so sore from the rope burns. Can you get some padding to put under my arms?"

"Yes," replied Ebed-Melech, "we thought of that. Here, catch!"

The rope and the rags to make pads for under his arms came snaking down into the dark. The men could not see where Jeremiah was, so the rope landed in the mud out of his reach. Poor Jeremiah thought, "I am so close to being saved, but I cannot reach the rope." He struggled to grab the rope which lay on top of the icky, sticky mud. Slowly but surely he got closer and closer. The mud got in his eyes and his ears and filled his beard and his hair. He tried to answer the men who were calling out to him, "How are you managing, Jeremiah? Should we start pulling on the ropes?" But when he opened his mouth the icky, sticky mud poured in and he swallowed some. *I'm going to keep my mouth shut!* he thought to himself.

After a long struggle, Jeremiah finally reached the rope and rags. He put the pads under his arms as best he could, then he looped the rope under his arms and around his back. "Pull!" he shouted to the men. The thirty men began to pull

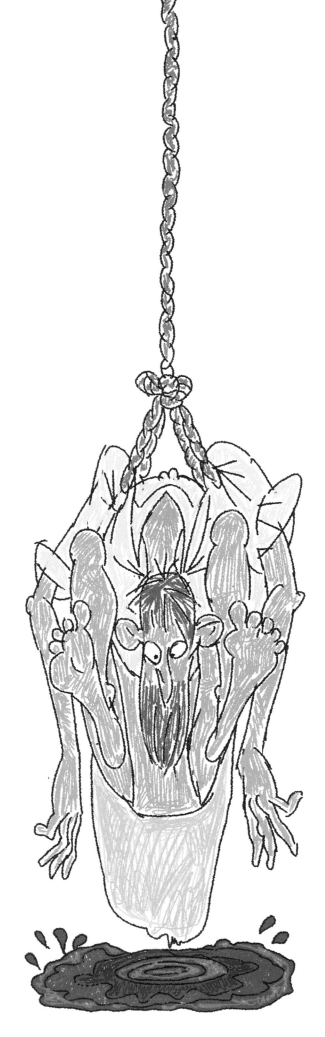

with all their strength. But the mud was very icky and very sticky and it did not want to let Jeremiah go. They pulled harder. The rope bit deeper into Jeremiah's arms even though he had the padding there. Slowly he felt himself being lifted out of the mud. First his chest came free. Then his waist. Then with a great big sucking sound his whole body was free, and he found himself hanging in midair. It was very uncomfortable, but he was free of the icky, sticky mud, and that was wonderful.

The men lifted him gently over the rim of the cistern. He was covered from head to foot with mud. His eyes and ears, his beard and hair, and even his mouth were full of icky, sticky mud. He didn't even look like Jeremiah. In fact, he looked so funny that even though the men were sorry for him they started to laugh. Jeremiah wondered why they were laughing, because he couldn't think of anything funny about his experience. So Ebed-Melech said, "Jeremiah, we're so happy you are safe. But you do look funny. You are a very icky, sticky prophet. Even your own mother would not recognize you right now!"

Jeremiah never laughed very much, but he laughed then. "You're right," he said, "and she would not be very pleased. She always told me to stay away from mud holes."

Jeremiah knew that people liked acting. So instead of preaching sermons all the time, he made up plays. God wrote the scripts for the plays and Jeremiah acted them out.

One day he put an oxen's yoke around his neck to get the people's attention. He wore the yoke for some time. It was a message to the people that they would not be free to live in Judah but would be ruled by the Babylonians.

Jeremiah & Me

Friends are very important. Jeremiah didn't have many good friends, but he did have a few who saved his life. It is very important to choose the sort of friends who won't run away when we get into trouble.

I'M GETTING A GREAT PICTURE OF YOUR TONGUE.

Your Family Video Theater

Little Brown Jugs

Jeremiah

Cast: Two little brown jugs named Jugular and Jugears;
  Mr. Potter

Scene: A shelf in the house of Mr. Potter.

Jugears	I wish I could get out of this place.
Jugular	Why? This is a comfortable shelf, and the room is warm.
Jugears	It's that potter's wheel. All day long. Clickety-clack. Clickety-clack. It drives me nuts.
Jugular	It doesn't bother me.
Jugears	Well, maybe it would if you listened.
Jugular	I do listen. Maybe everything is louder to you because of your big ears.
Jugears	That's not funny. You know I hate my ears.
Jugular	No point in hating them. You can't change them.
Jugears	Well, thanks!
Jugular	Mr. Potter knew what he was doing when he gave you big ears.
Jugears	I know that, and that's why I'm so angry at Mr. Potter.
Jugular	Well, if it weren't for Mr. Potter you wouldn't even be a jug, and you wouldn't be around to be angry.
Jugears	I guess you're right. But that doesn't answer the question of why he gave me these dumb ears.
Jugular	Look, he's taking a break from his wheel. Let's ask him.
Jugears	What's the point? He's not interested in us.
Jugular	How do you know that? I'll call him. Mr. Potter, could we have a word with you please?

Mr. Potter	Of course, you can have a word with me any time you want to. Call on me, and I'll answer you and show you things that you don't know.
Jugular	It's my friend, Jugears. He doesn't like the ears you gave him, and he wants to know why you did it. He feels silly because he doesn't look like the rest of us.
Jugears	That's right, Mr. Potter. It doesn't seem fair that you should make me look so weird.
Mr. Potter	Oh, my dear little Jugears, I'm so glad you asked me about this. Let me explain. I didn't give you silly ears. I made you with special handles.
Jugears	Well, they may be handles to you, but they're ears to me!
Mr. Potter	Okay, but I made you, so you should at least listen to what I had in mind when I made you.
Jugears	Well, why did you not make me like Jugular? I love his long slender neck, and I hate my big ears—er—handles.
Mr. Potter	Because Jugular here was made to hold flowers, and for that he needs a long neck. But you were specially ordered by a man who needs a jug to hold precious water. I made you with big handles so he could carry you.
Jugular	I'm glad you explained that. I thought I was better than old Jugears because I am prettier. But now I see I'm not better and he's not worse.
Jugears	You mean we're just different?
Mr. Potter	That's right. All the things I make are different because I need them to do different things.
Jugears	So what should we do, Mr. Potter?
Mr. Potter	I think you should decide to be the best carrier of precious water around these parts, Jugears.
Jugular	And I'll be the best flower-holding jug in the district.
Mr. Potter	That's all I want from both of you. That's why I made you the way I did.

Great is your faithfulness.

Lamentations 3:23

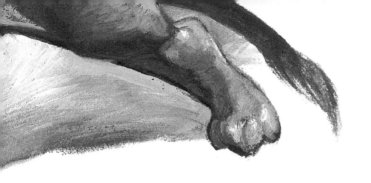

DANIEL

One day Daniel awoke to the sounds of fighting. The army of Nebuchadnezzar, king of Babylon, had surrounded Jerusalem. The people of God fought as well as they could, but the Babylonians overcame them. Many people of Judah died or were taken as prisoners to Babylon.

Nebuchadnezzar ordered the chief of his court officials to bring in some of the prisoners. He was looking for the best of the young men to serve him. The slaves had to be handsome, very clever, well informed, and know how to serve a king. The chief of Nebuchadnezzar's court chose some fine young men of Judah who had belonged to the royal household. Among them were four who were outstanding. Their names were Daniel, Hananiah, Mishael, and Azariah. These teenagers loved and served the one true God and had

been very sad to leave their country, their palace, and their temple, and to be taken away as slaves.

They went to school to learn the Babylonian language and customs and quickly rose to the top of their class. Daniel did the best, but God helped all of them to learn well. The chief officer who was in charge of them especially liked Daniel.

The young men from Judah did not want to eat the food they were given. It tasted very good and was supposed to make them healthy, but because this particular food had been offered to false gods before they got it, they knew God's law said they must not eat it. So Daniel asked the official for permission not to eat it.

"But what will you eat instead?" asked the surprised man.

"Just give us vegetables and water to drink," said Daniel.

How can I be brave like Daniel?

The man was amazed. The king's food that had been offered to idols was very rich and fancy. He couldn't imagine anyone choosing vegetables and water instead.

Daniel explained why they didn't want to eat the king's food. "If we ate it that would be like saying we believe in your gods, and we don't. We believe there is only one true God, and he is the one we worship." The official wanted very much to do what Daniel asked, but the king had commanded him to make sure that all the young men in training were the healthiest and most handsome men around. What would the king do to him if the young men from Judah looked skinny and miserable?

So Daniel went to the guard in charge and begged, "Feed us vegetables and water for ten days and see how we look." The guard agreed to do this experiment. At the end of the ten days the four friends looked far healthier than any of the young men who were eating the royal food, so the teenagers from Judah were allowed to eat what they wanted during the rest of their training time.

After three years, the young captives were brought before King Nebuchadnezzar to talk with him. It was sort of like an exam. The king was delighted with the four friends and said they were ten times better than all the other students and all the clever men and magicians in his whole kingdom. So Daniel and his three friends became the king's best servants.

As the years went by, the four men found it was sometimes dangerous to stay true to their God, especially when everyone around them was serving false gods. Once three friends of Daniel were thrown into a fiery furnace because they refused to worship an idol. But God saved them from the flames. It was a miracle, and King Nebuchadnezzar was so impressed with this that he decided to serve their God instead of his.

After Nebuchadnezzar died, Daniel served three other heathen rulers. God helped Daniel to do his job so well that at one time the other government leaders he was in charge of got very jealous. They set up a law that whoever did not bow only to the king would be thrown into a den of lions. They knew Daniel would never obey that law. But God saved Daniel just as he had saved his three friends from the fiery furnace.

The Bible tells us that God loved Daniel very much. God spoke to Daniel in dreams and visions and showed him what would happen in the future. Daniel was helped by God to stay true to him even when it was hard or dangerous to obey God. He knew Daniel would rather die than stop loving and serving him. Daniel brought great glory to God and is one of the greatest prophets in the Bible.

THIS IS A STORY TOLD AS FANTASY MARRIED TO FACT TO BE MIXED WITH FAITH AND LAUGHTER, LOVE AND JOY.

TIME FOR DIN-DIN. SAY AAAAAH!

Let's Pretend

THE PARTY

"Hurry up, Hananiah," Mishael said to his friend. "The party is well under way, and there's still lots of work to do."

Azariah ran into the kitchen to order some more food. He nearly upset the trays of wine and fruits his two friends were carrying to the guests.

"It's wild out there," Hananiah gasped.

"They are all drunk, and yet they order us to bring out more wine! Perhaps we should refuse," Mishael suggested.

"Remember what happened last time we did that," Hananiah reminded him. "We got thrown into the furnace."

"And that was King Nebuchadnezzar's doing," added Mishael. "His son, King Belshazzar, is far more wicked than he was. I can't imagine what he would do to us if we refuse to serve them."

"Wine! Where is the wine?" screamed a loud voice. The three friends stopped talking and headed out through the stone arch that led out of the kitchen into the banquet room. The scene was frightening. People were fighting, becoming sick, and doing dreadful things because they had had too much wine to drink and because it was their custom to do dreadful things.

As Hananiah brought the new wine up to the king's table, he suddenly saw the golden cups. He stopped in horror. Why, he knew where those cups had come

from. They had been taken from the temple in Jerusalem years ago when the people had all been captured and marched away to Babylon. They were holy cups, used by the priests in the worship of Jehovah. Now this wicked king was using them to get himself and his guests drunk and to honor his dreadful gods.

"Pour the wine! Pour the wine," the king demanded, holding out one of God's special cups. Hananiah couldn't do it. He wouldn't do it. He would die first. "I'm sor-sorry, your majesty," he stammered, "but I . . . I . . . can't . . . I won't . . ."

The king pushed aside his food, and the golden goblet fell to the floor with a crash. "How do you dare disobey me? I am Belshazzar, king of Babylon!" He began to shout at Hananiah, his voice getting louder and louder all the time.

By now Mishael and Azariah were at Hananiah's side. They would die with him. They knew that their God, Jehovah, could save them. But even if he chose not to, they would not do this dreadful thing the king asked of them. They would not make fun of the one true God they loved and served.

The king's face was turning purple, he was so angry. He was just about to order the three friends arrested and tortured in front of everyone at the party, when someone screamed. "Look! Look! Look at the wall!"

Everyone turned and looked at the huge white stone wall of the banquet room. "What . . . what is it?" whispered a court official.

"It's a . . . a . . . a hand," hissed the ruler of the feast, "or rather, f-fingers!

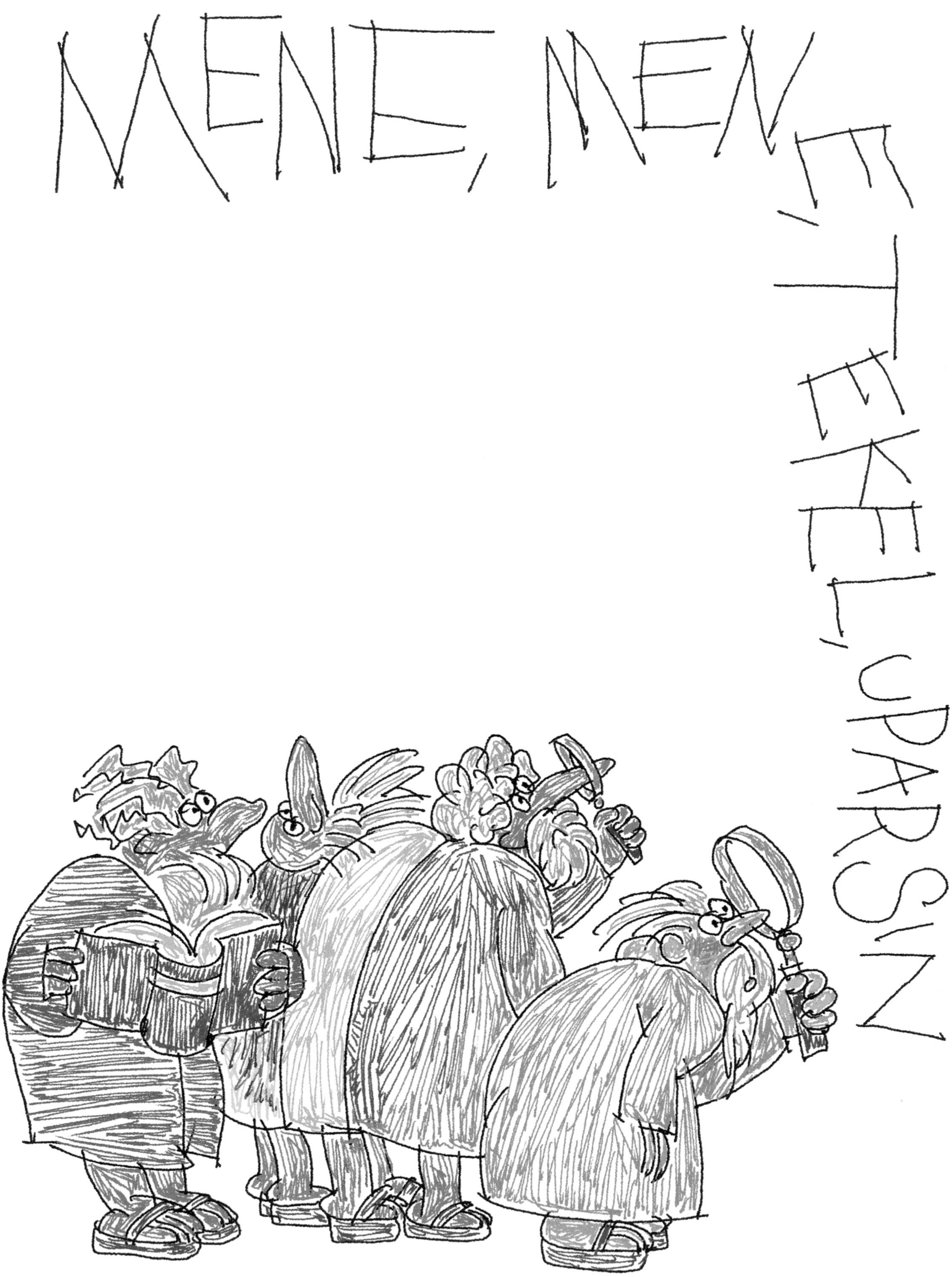
MENE, MENE, TEKEL, UPARSIN

Just a finger writing letters!" There was a deathly silence in the huge hall. Even the drunkest guest was gazing at the wall. The hand began to write. There were gasps. Some of the women fainted, but no one took any notice of them.

The king watched the hand, and now his face was no longer purple with rage, it was as white as a sheet. His knees began to knock together, he was so frightened. The king forgot all about the three disobedient slaves, Mishael, Hananiah, and Azariah. He shouted out for his wise men. "Magicians, astrologers, wise men, come and tell me what this strange writing means!" he ordered. The words were in a strange language that no one in the room could understand.

The wise men of Babylon pressed forward till they could see the writing on the wall clearly. But they couldn't read it. At that, King Belshazzar became more frightened than ever. Then everyone began to talk at once. They made such a noise that Belshazzar's mother heard the rumpus and came to see what was happening. When she heard the story and looked at the writing on the wall, she knew it was God's writing. So she told her son to send for Daniel, who in the time of Belshazzar's father, Nebuchadnezzar, had been able to find out what God's words meant. Mishael, Hananiah, and Azariah clapped their hands. They had been saved from death once again, but this time they knew that God was going to punish the wicked king.

Daniel came into the party room, and the three friends prayed that God would

tell him what the words meant. The king begged him to read the writing, even though he was scared to know what it said. He knew that the great God his father had come to believe in, the God he had ridiculed and ignored, had sent him a message. "If you can read this writing," he told Daniel, "I'll give you new clothes and a gold chain and make you the third most important ruler in the land."

"Keep your gifts. I don't want them," Daniel retorted, "but I'll read the writing for you and tell you what it means." Then he told the wicked son of King Nebuchadnezzar that when God had spoken to his father, his father had believed and had been very sorry for all his sins. "You know all this, Belshazzar," he said, "but unlike your father, you set yourself up against the one true God and tried to fight him. Now God has sent you a message. This is what it is. Your reign is over, you are lost, and tonight enemies will take the city and kill you."

Belshazzar knew Daniel was telling the truth, so he rewarded him and made him an important person in the kingdom. But just as God had said, that very night the king was killed and a new king took over.

Daniel and his three friends talked together till the early morning hours. "How great is our God," they said, and they promised each other they would serve him forever, whatever lay ahead for them under the new conqueror that God had sent to punish Belshazzar. "We will stay true to Jehovah," they said. And so they did as long as they lived.

Have you ever had a bad dream? King Nebuchadnezzar had a terrible one. It was so weird! He tried to discover the meaning of it so he called together all his wise men and magicians. The king would not tell them what his dream was. No one

83

could tell him his dream or the meaning of his dream. Finally he asked Daniel. Daniel and his three friends prayed about it, and God revealed the dream and the meaning of the dream to Daniel.

Daniel said to the king: "In the middle of the night you dreamed about a great and mighty statue with a terrifying appearance."

This is how Daniel described the statue:

Its head was made of gold.

Its chest and arms were silver.

Its belly and thighs were made of bronze.

Its legs were made of iron.

Its feet were made of both iron and clay.

But there was more to the dream. Suddenly a great boulder crashed down the mountainside and shattered the feet of the statue.

The image was top heavy because the heaviest metal was on the top. When its feet shattered, the statue crashed so hard that it crumbled into a powder so fine that the wind blew it away.

Something happened to the boulder too. It grew and grew until it became a huge mountain and filled the whole earth! Daniel told the king that the boulder was a picture of the power of God's kingdom.

85

Daniel & Me

Have you ever felt lonely because the other kids you were playing with were doing something wrong and you didn't want to do it? But you didn't want to be different from the other kids either. You knew you believed in God and should obey him and that seemed so hard to do. It would be so much easier to do the things the other kids were doing. When you feel that way, ask God to help you to be strong and kind and also to take away your lonely feelings.

Daniel knew what he should do and what he should not do because he knew what God's law said. If you read the Bible, it will tell you the things you are not supposed to do and, maybe even more important,

what you should do for God. In the New Testament, Jesus made these things clear in his teachings, and so did Paul in his letters to the new Christian churches.

Maybe you don't like the idea of eating vegetables. You'd rather eat ice cream or chocolate. Sometimes you have to eat foods that make you healthy instead of eating junk food. And you have to do things you don't enjoy doing very much because they are right or because they will help others understand God better. One day God may send you as a missionary to a place where they eat mainly rice, for instance, and there is no ice cream or chocolate. Would you be willing to do it for him?

Let's Make a Video about

I LOST MY SPOON! ANYBODY SEE MY SPOON?

Your Family Video Theater

Little Lion

Daniel

Cast: Mother Lion, Little Lion, Father Lion, Cousin Lion, Daniel, King, angel, soldiers

Scene: A lions' den.

Narrator	Little Lion was hungry. It had been a long time since he had a good meal. He tried to go to sleep, but his mother pushed him away when he laid his head on her paws.
Mother Lion	I'm hungry too. Don't crowd me, Little Lion. The keepers are punishing us for some reason.
Little Lion	What have we done, Mother? I hate this place. Why, oh, why did the Lion Maker let us be put in this dreadful, dirty, old cave?
Mother Lion	We mustn't question the Lion Maker, my son. He would have us roam free. But the men he made have become evil and cruel.
Little Lion	Will they starve us to death?
Mother Lion	I don't know, Little Lion. It's many days now since they have given us any food.
Narrator	Little Lion began to cry. Great big tears ran down his mane and splashed onto his floppy paws.
Little Lion	I think it's unfair! Next time a keeper comes, I will growl at him and frighten him away.
Mother Lion	Little Lion, maybe the Lion Maker is teaching us self-control. It's hard to be patient when you're a lion and you are hungry.
Little Lion	I don't want to learn self-control. I want some lunch!
Narrator	But there was no meat for the starving lions that night or

87

the next or the next, and the animals grew desperate. One day the lions heard the sound of voices approaching their cave, and the animals got to their feet. They were sure a meal was coming. But it was only the soldiers with a prisoner, an old man called Daniel.

Soldier	Daniel, will you worship only King Darius and no other god during the rest of the month?
Daniel	No, I will not. I serve Jehovah. He is the only one I worship, for he is the one and only true God. Even if you throw me into the lions' den, I will remain true to my God.
Father Lion	How cruel these people are. Daniel is an old man. I have heard of him. He has served the Lion Maker all his life and loves him greatly.
Little Lion	But, Mother, you said the Lion Maker loves us too. Perhaps he has given us our lunch, although the old man looks pretty tough.
Narrator	As the soldiers gave Daniel a hard shove into the cave of the lions, the very hungry animals licked their lips. They were not in the habit of eating man meat, but they were half crazed with lack of food. Little Lion wondered what was going to happen. A big rock was rolled over the opening to the cave.
Father Lion	Fellow lions! We cannot attack this good man. Why, he has stood alone for God all his life.
Cousin Lion	But why then does God allow him to be thrown into our den? Perhaps he has fallen out of favor with the Lord, so it must be all right to gobble him up.
Mother Lion	But what if we crunched up God's prophet and *then* found out that God had sent him to us so we could look after him?
Little Lion	Look! There in the corner of the den—a bright light.
Mother Lion	It's an angel.
Father Lion	Now we know we mustn't touch Daniel. The Lion Maker has sent his angel to take care of his servant.
Narrator	Little Lion went up to the angel. When he was near, he knelt down on his wobbly knees. He was so weak from lack of food he could hardly walk.
Little Lion	Dear angel, I am so afraid I'll do something foolish. Please, could you bind my mouth tightly shut so I will not touch Daniel?

Angel	(smiling) If you wish.
Narrator	The angel took out some bright heavenly material and lovingly bound Little Lion's mouth tightly shut. He was glad that the small animal was so eager to do what was right. As the angel touched Little Lion an amazing thing happened. Little Lion didn't feel as hungry as he had. Perhaps wanting to please the Lion Maker had made him forget all about food, for Little Lion was suddenly quite content.
	Early in the morning Little Lion was awakened from a sound and peaceful sleep by footsteps and the sound of men moving something heavy. He opened one eye to the gray dawn, then the other as he saw the king at the opening of the cave.
King	Daniel, has your God whom you continually serve been able to rescue you from the lions?
Daniel	Yes, King Darius. The angel of the Lord shut their mouths, and they have not hurt me. You know I never did anything wrong to you, O King.
King	Daniel! I'm overjoyed! I knew your God would save you. The jealous servants tricked me into making that law. Now they will be punished. Soldiers! Lift my friend gently from this pit. Come, Daniel. We shall have breakfast while I write a song of praise to your God.
Narrator	When Daniel had gone, the angel unbound Little Lion's mouth and disappeared.
Little Lion	It's a good thing we didn't gobble up Daniel, Mother. If we had, the king would not have been converted.
Narrator	That day the keepers brought the lions a big meal, and life was back to normal again.

THE ANGEL, MY GOD SENT HIS ANGEL, AND HE SHUT THE MOUTHS OF THE LIONS. Daniel 6:22

JONAH

Prophets were not perfect. Some prophets were not always happy. One prophet, Jonah, was very unhappy because God told Jonah to do something Jonah did not want to do. God told him to travel to the great city of Nineveh and preach to the people there. You would think Jonah would have been pleased to be asked by God to do such an important job. Jonah did not want to preach to the people of Nineveh because he did not like them. They were the enemies of Jonah's people and were very cruel. The Bible calls them violent. Jonah thought that if he preached to them, God would bless them. Then they would become stronger and make life more dangerous for Jonah and his people. Jonah really wanted God to punish them.

Rather than go to Nineveh as he was told, Jonah went on a ship that was sailing in another direction. It was going to the city of Tarshish. God was not going to let Jonah go as easily as that. God sent a big storm. The huge waves hit the ship hard and it was beginning to sink in the rough water. The sailors found out that the storm had been sent because Jonah was running away from God. When Jonah was asked about this, he could not tell a lie and told them the whole story. The sailors asked Jonah what they should do, and he said, "You'd better throw me overboard." He was an unhappy prophet. The sailors were good men and did not want to throw Jonah into the sea. They tried very hard to row their ship to land but were unable to do so. So they threw Jonah over the side. He sank down into the roaring waves. He was a very unhappy prophet.

But God had not finished with Jonah. He sent a very special fish with a large mouth to catch Jonah before he hit the bottom, and for three days and three nights Jonah spent a very uncomfortable and smelly time inside the big fish's tummy. Jonah thought being inside the fish was better than being drowned, but not much better. He was a very, very unhappy prophet. Soon he remembered to pray. God had been waiting to hear from Jonah and was pleased when Jonah finally got in touch with him, so God directed the fish to throw up Jonah safe and sound, but sore and smelly, on dry land.

"Now go to Nineveh," God said to him. This time Jonah did not argue. He did as he was told, arrived in Nineveh and preached God's message of warning to the people, telling them to change their ways. (Jonah was hoping they wouldn't listen to him.) They did what Jonah did not want them to do. They heard what God said, believed, changed, and were blessed. Strange as it may seem, Jonah, instead of being glad, was now a very, very, very unhappy prophet.

The weather was hot in Nineveh, and this made Jonah very, very, very, very unhappy. God prepared a special plant that grew quickly and gave Jonah some welcome shade. At last Jonah was happy about something. But not for long. God sent a worm that ate his plant, and the sun beat down on Jonah's head once more. This made Jonah a very, very, very, very, very unhappy prophet.

That's a lot of unhappy for one little prophet!

God spoke to Jonah and said, "Jonah, you are unhappy about many things. You are even upset with me about a little plant, yet you don't care about all these people. But I do, and you must learn to be interested in what I am concerned about or you will always be an unhappy prophet."

In trouble I cried to the Lord and he answered me.
Jonah 2:2 TLB

Let's **Pretend**

WALLY THE WHALE

THIS IS A STORY TOLD AS FANTASY MARRIED TO FACT TO BE MIXED WITH FAITH AND LAUGHTER, LOVE AND JOY.

ZZZZZZZ ZZZZZ ZZ!

Wally was a big fish. Even when he was a young baby he was a big fish. He had a long body, shiny and black like well-polished shoes. He had a great tail like the tail of a giant airplane. And he had a big mouth. His mouth was so big that the other fish used to say, "He'll swallow anything that gets in his way." So even the other big fish kept out of Wally's way. Wally liked that. He swam alone and did what he wanted to do. Nobody bothered him. Wally had a squeaky voice. All fish have squeaky voices, and they don't mind. But Wally thought that because he was the biggest fish in the sea he should have a deep voice. So he practiced hard to make his voice deep and strong.

Wally lived in a great sea sometimes called the "Sea in the Middle of the Earth." It wasn't really, but people thought it was, and so did Wally. He was the biggest fish in the middle of the earth. Wally swam from one end of the sea to the other. He swam past Tarshish and watched the people lying on the beach and fishing from their boats. He thought to himself, "These earth people can't swim like me. They are very small. If one of them got in my way, I could swallow him up in no time and have him for breakfast." Then with a splash of his mighty tail he would dive deep in the water. He liked to splash his tail where the earth people could see him. It made him feel very big and strong, and he hoped they were impressed.

Sometimes he swam past Joppa at the other end of the sea. There he watched the ships sail for faraway places like Tarshish. When the sea was nice and calm, he would dive deep down where the sun did not shine. There he would see with his special eyes the flat fish that lived in the dark and moved quietly among the weeds and the reefs. He was careful not to hit a reef because he knew that because he was so big he could cut himself badly on the sharp coral. If he did, those nasty sharks might come, and hundreds of them

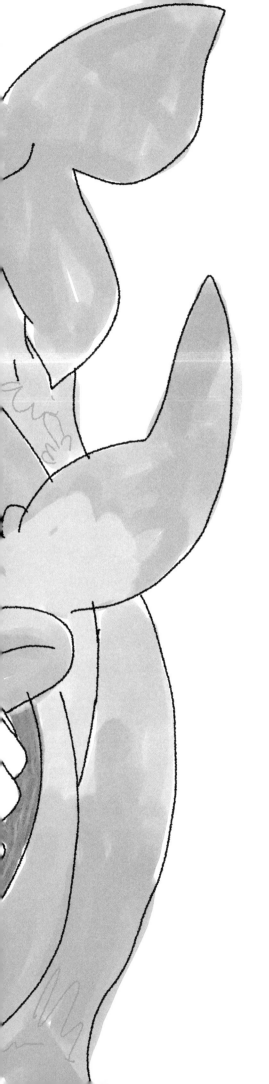

would attack him. He thought he was big enough to fight them off. But he wasn't too sure. A mighty flick of his tail stirred up the sand on the sea floor and sent the flat fish into hiding behind the coral where he could not come. Wally headed for the surface. Up into the light blue water where the sun shone and the families of shiny silver fish swam past as if in a hurry to go somewhere. Up into the light green water where tiny fish, pink, orange, and bright blue, darted and played in the warm sunlit water. Up past the bottom of the old ship sailing from Joppa, until he broke through the surface and sailed high into the air. He saw the sailors on the ship look at him as his great shiny black body rose high above them. Then he turned on his side and landed with such a great splash on the water that he sent a big wave onto the ship. The sailors rushed for safety and the ship almost sank. Wally smiled to himself as he went down into the depths again thinking, "Am I not the greatest fish in the Middle-of-the-Earth Sea? Am I not the greatest?"

One day the sea was no longer calm. A great storm had blown over the water. The wind was howling and the waves were building up as high as a house. Wally liked to stay deep under the surface when storms came, but he needed to breathe, so he came up quite often. Once when he did this he saw a strange sight. A ship of Joppa, the one he liked to splash, was rolling in the waves. The sails were torn and the waves were breaking over the sides of the ship. The sailors were in the stern of the ship holding an earth man by his arms and his legs. They seemed to be playing a game. Wally dove down and then came back to the surface in time to see the earth man thrown high in the air. With his arms and legs waving around like those of a rag doll thrown out of a playpen, the man sailed high in the air and with a splash disappeared under the water.

Wally hit the water with his great tail. In a flash he swam to the place where the earth man had gone under the waves. Down, down, down he went until he saw the earth man in the deep blue water where the flat fishes looked at him in surprise. Wally swam to the earth man, whose body was quite limp, and with his great teeth grabbed his clothes and headed for the surface. Up, up he went, hoping he would be in time before the earth man drowned. When he got to the surface, he was surprised to see that the storm had gone, the sea was calm. Wally knew that he could not stay above the surface very long because he would burn his shiny back. But he also knew that he could not stay under the water or the earth man would drown. He had an idea. He took a great gulp of air, threw the earth man in the air, caught him in his great big mouth, dove down deep, and swam as quickly as he could for the shore. Earth man had air to breathe and Wally was able to swim quickly in the deep water.

All went well until earth man began to wake up. He struggled to his feet wondering where on earth—or sea—he was. Wally's mouth was very big and very slippery. Earth man, whose name was Jonah, began to slide down Wally's throat. He tried to grab on to anything he could, but everything was wet and slippery. With a final rush he shot down Wally's throat into the big fish's belly. There he landed softly among the leftovers from Wally's lunch. Wally had eaten his lunch quickly, so there was plenty of air down there, and although it was smelly, it was warm. Jonah didn't know what to do. Then he remembered that he had not prayed for a long time. So he knelt down as best he could, told the Lord he was sorry he had been disobedient, and asked God to please get him out of that mess.

Wally didn't know what to do either. So for three days and three nights he kept swimming toward the shore. But he didn't know what he would do when he got there. Then he remembered that when his grandmother was very old and weak, she swam as hard as she could onto a beach and died there. Wally didn't want to do that but he thought he could get very close to a beach and somehow get the earth man out of his stomach. A growing ache in his stomach made him swim faster.

Then he had a great idea. As he came near to the beach, taking great care not to get caught on dry land, he took a great gulp of air into his stomach and made the biggest, deepest sound in fish history. No little squeak came from his throat. A mighty deep note rang from deep inside him. Jonah was suddenly caught up in a great rush of wind that pushed him up Wally's throat, past his giant tonsils, through his great mouth, past his awesome teeth, and high into the air. He saw the water beneath him and then he landed with a splat on the wet sand. He lay there a long time. Wally swam anxiously around until he saw Jonah stagger to his feet. Then he splashed his great tail and dove deep down among the flat fish.

For the first time in his life Wally had done something really useful. Now he knew why he had been given such a big mouth, why he had learned to practice a deep voice, and why he could dive deep and flip high in the air. God had made him just right for the work he wanted Wally to do. The flat fish saw Wally smile as he swam past, and the cold eyes of the sharks watched in wonder.

Jonah & Me

What do you do when you are sorry? Do you try to tell someone you are sorry? People have different ways of telling people they are sorry. Sometimes you can give someone a hug or a kiss. Or maybe you can write a note instead of saying something. When the people in Nineveh were sorry they had been cruel and wanted to tell God they were very sorry, they put on sackcloth (very rough cloth) and sat in ashes. That must have been uncomfortable, don't you think? They even put sackcloth on their donkeys and other animals! How we say we are sorry isn't the most important thing. The most important thing is to say it and mean it. Think of some of the ways you say you are sorry. What are they?

tuff Neat stuff Neat

Nineveh had such wide walls around the city that seven chariots could ride side by side on top of the walls. Do you know what a chariot is? It's a horse-drawn, two-wheeled cart, with room for the driver to stand on the floor of the cart.

The city of Nineveh had zoos, orchards, and parks outside the city walls.

The people of Nineveh had pure water to drink. It came from mountains fifty miles away from the city. Something special was used to bring the water to the city. Do you know what it was?

THE THROAT IN THIS FISH COSTUME IS MUCH BIGGER AND ROOMIER.

QUIET, EVERYBODY! **QUIET!** WE'RE MAKIN' A MOVIE.

INSECTICIDE PICTURES

IT WAS NOT A WHALE!

'TWAS SO A WHALE!

'TWASN'T

'TWAS!

'TWASN'T

'TWAS!

'TWASN'T

Let's Make a Video about

The Seagulls

Cast: Two seagulls, Bea Gull and Dee Gull

Scene: High in the rigging of the good ship Albatross somewhere in the middle of the Middle-of-the-Earth Sea.

Bea	I'm tired out.
Dee	Me too. It's a long way from land, and this is the worst storm I've ever flown in.
Bea	This old ship looks as if it won't make it. But I surely was glad to see it. At least we can take a break from flying for a few hours.
Dee	Unless it sinks!
Bea	If it does, at least we can fly. We're not like these earth people. They can't fly, and most of them can't swim.
Dee	I think they would all like to change places with us right now.
Bea	Sure. But I wouldn't mind borrowing one of their bunks for an hour or two instead of sitting on this swaying masthead.

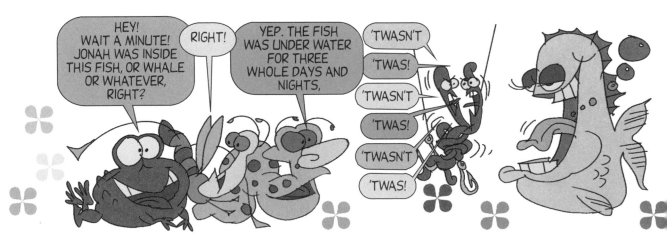

Dee	Why are we flying all the way to Italy anyway?
Bea	To see our relatives, of course. It's been so long since I've seen them. I doubt if I'll recognize them.
Dee	You'll recognize Cousin Lee Gull. There's only one beak in the world like his.
Bea	That's true. But what about little Wee Gull? Last time we were in Italy he was just an egg.
Dee	I'm hungry. I wish the cook would throw out some scraps.
Bea	Look, they're getting ready to throw out something now.
Dee	I don't believe it. No scraps. That's a man! They're not going to throw him overboard, are they?
Bea	I don't know what that little fellow has done, but they are certainly upset with him.
Dee	Shh. What are they saying?
Bea	Something about the storm being all his fault.
Dee	He's admitting it. Something about him running away from the Lord.
Bea	This is weird! He's telling them to throw him overboard.
Dee	Yeah, but look. They don't want to do it.
Bea	Well, would you throw somebody into that sea? He won't last ten seconds.
Dee	Look! They're praying!
Bea	In all my years hitching rides on ships, I've never seen sailors pray before.
Dee	What are they saying?

Bea	They're asking the Lord to forgive them if they are doing something they shouldn't. But this man says he's the Lord's prophet and it will be all right if they throw him overboard.
Dee	Do you believe that?
Bea	Why not?
Dee	Well, I don't. You're gullible.
Bea	Maybe I am. But if he's the Lord's prophet, the Lord will look after him.
Dee	Even if he's running away from the Lord?
Bea	Maybe this is the Lord's way of stopping him from running away.
Dee	It will surely work. There's nowhere to run where he's going. I hope he can swim!
Bea	Look out! There he goes.
Dee	Can you see him?
Bea	No. He sank like a stone. He'll never survive in that sea.
Dee	That's strange. The storm just stopped. The sea is calm.
Bea	Look! Over there, where the sun is glowing red on the water. What is it?
Dee	It's the biggest fish I've ever seen.
Bea	And what's that in its mouth?
Dee	Oh, no! It's the prophet.
Bea	This is amazing. It looks as if the fish is trying to rescue him.
Dee	How in the world is he going to do that?
Bea	I don't know, but there's a look in his great fishy eye that makes me think he knows what he's doing.

Dee	You know what? I think he just swallowed the prophet. I guess that's the end of him.
Bea	Somehow, I don't think so.
Dee	You don't? Well, what do you think?
Bea	I think that the Lord caught up with his runaway prophet, turned him around, and arranged for him to get back to land.
Dee	Seems like an awful lot of trouble for the Lord.
Bea	He goes to a lot of trouble to see that all of us do what he wants us to do.
Dee	If that prophet ever gets to land, I know one thing. He'll never run away again!

Head for the Setting Sun

Words and Music by
STUART BRISCOE and LARRY MOORE

BETWEEN THE OLD & NEW TESTAMENT

More than four hundred years passed after the books of the Old Testament were written and before the books of the New Testament were put together. These are called "the silent years" because God was not speaking to his people, the Jews, through prophets like Isaiah and Jeremiah anymore. Many bad things were happening to the Jews. Their homeland, Palestine, was invaded by cruel armies. Some wicked men who ignored God did things that they should not have done. One of these cruel men was a high priest named Alexander. The people hated him so they threw oranges and lemons at him. Alexander was furious and called for the soldiers to kill many people. The Jews longed for a brave person to come and deliver them from their enemies. The Jews believed that God had promised to send them a deliverer called "Messiah."

One brave Jew named Judas Maccabeus (his name means *hammer*) and a few of his

108

friends were able to overthrow the cruel rulers for a short time. This gave the Jews hope. Soon the rulers regained power and were just as cruel as ever. So the Jews kept on looking for a savior.

King Herod, who had built a beautiful temple in Jerusalem, was sitting in his palace

earth and that is why they did not listen to Jesus or follow him. A few people listened to Jesus, loved him, and became his disciples. Later they were called *Christians*.

After Jesus went back to heaven, the Christians told each other true stories and teachings they remembered about Jesus. As

one day when some wise men from the East told him that a "King of the Jews" had just been born. Herod was in a panic because he knew the Jews would want this new king to overthrow him and keep his sons and grandsons named Herod from being kings. So he decided to kill this baby king and ordered all baby boys in Bethlehem to be murdered. Herod did not understand that Jesus, the "King of the Jews," had come to save people from their sins, not to start a war. Many people did not understand why Jesus came to

time went on, the Christians thought it would be a good idea to write down these stories. Four men, Matthew, Mark, Luke, and John, collected the stories. We call these writings the *Gospels.* Later when there were many more Christians, the leaders of the churches, especially Paul, Peter, and John, wrote letters to them. We call these letters the *Epistles.* After many years, these stories and letters were collected from different places and put together to make the New Testament.

These innovative books will appeal to parents who want to teach biblical truths to their children in a fresh and exciting way. The interactive presentation of Bible stories, using songs, drama, and cartoons, makes the **B.I.B.L.E.** books ideal for family devotions. Kids will actually look forward to spending time together learning about God's word. No more coaxing and cajoling.

This multi-media approach can add excitement and enrichment to other educational settings:

- Home school
- Christian school
- Children's church
- Sunday school

Songs and readings from these books are also available on audio.

Six adventures are waiting in each book of the **B.I.B.L.E.** series. Take an excursion with your family from creation through the New Testament. Look below at characters and events found in all four books:

$14.99 each • Hardback • 112 pages

Moses Takes a Road Trip
And Other Famous Journeys

- *Creation*
- *Adam and Eve*
- *Noah*
- *Abram*
- *Moses*
- *Joshua*

ISBN 0-8010-4183-X

Jesus Makes a Major Comeback
And Other Amazing Feats

- *John the Baptist*
- *Jesus' Birth*
- *Jesus' Miracles*
- *Jesus' Big Week*
- *Jesus' Resurrection*
- *Luke*

ISBN 0-8010-4197-X

David Drops a Giant Problem
And Other Fearless Heroes

- *Samuel*
- *David*
- *Solomon*
- *Jeremiah*
- *Daniel*
- *Jonah*

ISBN 0-8010-4216-X

Paul Hits the Beach
And Other Wild Adventures

- *Peter*
- *Paul's Life*
- *Paul's Journeys*
- *Timothy*
- *James*
- *John*

ISBN 0-8010-4202-X

BAKER
INTERACTIVE
BOOKS FOR
Li*VELY*
EDUCATION

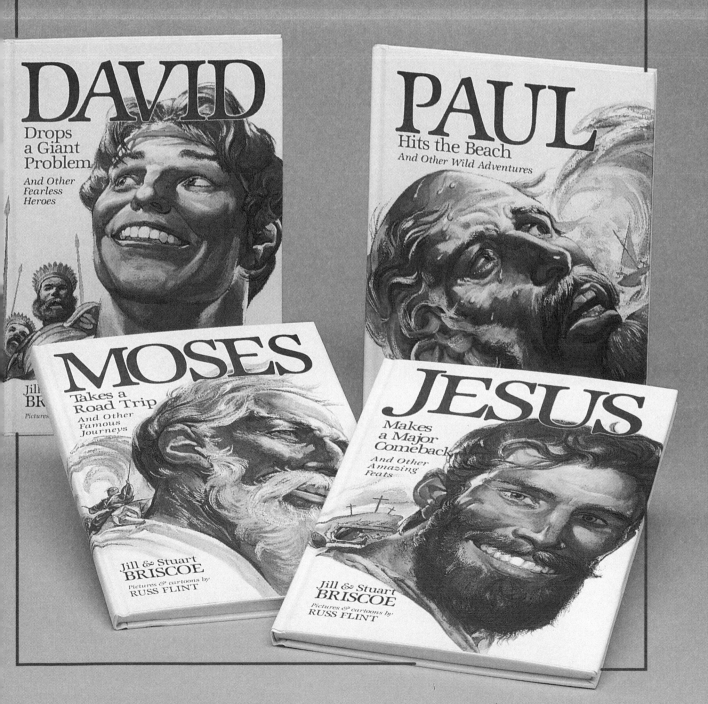

Jill and **Stuart Briscoe** are the parents of three grown children and the grandparents of nine. Jill has written more than forty books, and Stuart more than fifty. Stuart serves as senior pastor of Elmbrook Church in Brookfield, Wisconsin. Jill is an advisor to women's ministries at the church, and director of Telling the Truth media and ministries. Both are worldwide speakers at retreats and conferences. The Briscoes live in Oconomowoc, Wisconsin.

Russ Flint is the designer/illustrator of many children's books, including *Let's Make a Memory, Let's Hide a Word, My Very First Bible,* and *Teach Me About Jesus.* He regularly contributes artwork to such magazines as *Ideals* and *Guideposts for Kids* and is co-founder of Dayspring Card Company. He has also illustrated such familiar classics as *Legend of Sleepy Hollow, A Christmas Carol, Swan Lake,* and *Little Women.* He lives in Greenville, California.

How can I be brave like Daniel?

Why is it good that God sees everything?

Would you like wisdom or lots of money?